I0066609

All rights reserved
Copyright © Robert Julian, 2025

The right of Robert Julian to be identified as the author of this
work has been asserted in accordance with Section 78
of the Copyright, Designs and Patents Act 1988

The book cover is copyright to Robert Julian

This book is published by
Grosvenor House Publishing Ltd
Link House
140 The Broadway, Tolworth, Surrey, KT6 7HT.
www.grosvenorhousepublishing.co.uk

This book is sold subject to the conditions that it shall not, by way of
trade or otherwise, be lent, resold, hired out or otherwise circulated
without the author's or publisher's prior consent in any form of
binding or cover other than that in which it is published and
without a similar condition including this condition being
imposed on the subsequent purchaser.

A CIP record for this book
is available from the British Library

Paperback ISBN 978-1-83615-408-2

Contents

In earlier centuries, the rules and aims of trade were largely tied to power relationships between countries and nation-building.

The 1930s is an era frequently referenced in relation to trade issues, and the writings of J. M. Keynes provide his understanding and opinions, from which rules can be drawn.

> • Rule 1: Imbalances and lack of reciprocity matter first and foremost. • Rule 2: Tariffs were more a symptom than a cause of the Great Depression. • Rule 3: Tariffs are sometimes justified if your aims match improving international equilibrium. • Rule 4: Throughout Keynes' writing on tariffs and protection, he always warned of their pitfalls and dangers.

Game Theory type thinking can help to explain why free trade rules are at the same time both desirable, and yet need agreements and negotiations to make countries follow the rules.

The Bretton Woods rules, structures, and institutions, sought to create a bias towards more trade, and more support to help countries with crises in trade and other international financial flows.

Alternative economists believe the rules of free trade ideology focus only on present economic capabilities, and neglect how countries have always used industrial policies to develop their economies.

CHAPTER TWO: China puts the Existing Rules-Based Trading System Under Pressure.

Many other countries before China used industrial policies, but China is a much larger country, and is not converging either in political values or its economic norms and structures.

Subsidies are a big issue for China's trading partners, leading to the related dispute over whether China's State Owned Enterprises can be considered 'Public Bodies' that give out subsidies.

Another contention is the way China has used 'Forced Technology Transfer', to gain manufacturing knowledge and capability from developed country companies wishing to sell into China.

China's opaque structures and the lack of delineation between its ever more pervasive government and commercial activity make proving breaches of the rules difficult.

The first Trump administration departed from the norms of the WTO, and instead acted and negotiated on trade issues unilaterally and more assertively.

The Biden administration maintained the stance of Trump's trade policies, but with more emphasis on subsidies rather than further tariff threats, and with more emphasis on gaining allies abroad.

The traditional argument of the free-market economist is that governments have a poor record of 'picking winners', but for China, 'Green' sectors have been a good bet.

Globalisation was attractive to developed countries and their voters, when they thought they were the only ones who could do high-end manufacturing, but it is getting harder to maintain this role.

The car industry is a key desirable economic sector that developed countries will be unwilling to lose to China, illustrating why protectionism is back on the political agenda.

China seemed to be the ideal outsourcing manufacturing location for Apple who got rich: But Apple might turn out to have been lured into the biggest example of technology transfer in history.

Export-led growth based on increasing manufacturing competence has been the main route to economic development, but now China and de-industrialisation trends are making this harder.

China is likely to dominate certain economic sectors where its industrial policies are effective, and yet the flaws of its economic system mean it will still fall short of true economic success.

A harmonious trading system has reciprocity and symmetry, while distortions leading to surpluses and deficits cause disharmony: Look at the trade statistics and not the rhetoric.

Hayek made the strongest arguments regarding the dangers of governments making 'arbitrary' decisions to protect certain groups against the distribution mechanisms of free markets.

Industrial and protectionist policies, with their arbitrary rules and judgments, require high-quality, benevolent government personnel and increase the scope for corruption.

The efficiency and economies of scale in the supply chains and production processes of factories have played a large role in creating affluent countries: Protectionist trade policies can harm this.

The plan has some desirable automatic market mechanisms, which reduces the need for arbitrary decisions from politicians and bureaucrats implicit in other protectionist approaches.

It is important to differentiate between different traded goods when considering industrial or protectionist policies, including the attributes of the products, their production, and their markets.

At any one period in time, there will always be 'Prize Sector' economic activities which are extra desirable to have, and therefore trade policy surrounding these sectors will be more contentious.

Protectionist policies are rightly accused of harming economic growth, but growth is not everything, as inequality and jobs can matter more, and also growth puts more pressure on the environment.

What an ideal utopian trading system might look like, if an all-knowing economist God could create and enforce complex rules and categorisations for traded goods.

The second Trump administration is going hard into using tariffs, creating much uncertainty for business, losing the moral high ground, and in danger of making the US look just as bad as China.

Introduction

The rich and developed countries of the world are usually identified with two broad labels, which together provide a shorthand for understanding both their political systems and their economic systems. First, the label of being a 'liberal democracy' signifies a collection of values, norms, and rights on the political side. Then the key economic label, which is usually paired with the liberal democracy label, is to be called a 'free market economy'. This highlights that it is an ingrained assumption that to be an economically developed, sophisticated and affluent country goes hand in hand with accepting the merits of free markets and free trade. Together, this shorthand pairing of political and economic 'rules' has defined for the last few generations what it is to be in the most desirable and developed group of countries.

One could claim that the liberal democracy side of this label is followed in a more or less absolute and unwavering way in all developed countries, and their histories show a trend of ever more comprehensive and more sophisticated rules and practices, in areas like human rights, freedom of speech, and democracy. But, while the free market side of the label is relatively guaranteed and unwavering in the domestic sphere, the rules regarding the free international trade part of the label have never been adhered to in such an absolute way, and especially in recent years, have not shown the forward direction of travel towards a consensus, compared to the rules in the political sphere. In other words, the rules and ideals of international trade are still not yet properly nailed down, and a large amount of difference of opinion and subjectivity remain in this complex area.

If challenged, the politicians in most developed countries and even most other countries around the world would reply with a short sound bite in praise of the merits of free trade. But for something so universally praised and referenced, the rules, ideals and assumptions regarding free trade have been periodically overruled and ignored surprisingly often. As is human nature, a political fudge has coexisted alongside intellectual idealism over free trade questions. A seemingly dominant economic ideology based on the benefits of free trade rules is or was the headline or nominal policy, but it always existed alongside persistent de facto examples of political expediency, where governments saw fit ignoring or cheating on this ideology. This fudge has allowed rich Western countries to tick along reasonably happily for the last few decades, without their beliefs or policies in this area really being scrutinised. But this was until the discomfort of the massive challenge from China exporting on a frightening scale, revealed how conditional and easily shaken their nominal commitment to free trade rules really is. As I was completing this essay, President Trump won a second term in the US and quickly brought tariffs and protectionist trade policies into the centre of world news, emphasising this point.

If the logical collection of rules suggested by free trade theory no longer even loosely tether the leading economic countries to its ideology, what are the significant rules that either can survive this change, or can be agreed upon to guide countries and policymakers in this policy world cast adrift from free trade concepts? This essay aims to look at the history and nature of these explicit and implicit rules surrounding international trade, to shed more light on why rules and practices have not been nailed down, and to think about the many dissonances and subtleties that escape the usual simplistic debates. The result reveals the multidimensional nature of this subject, which unfortunately singularly fails to give up comprehensive answers or neat conclusions. However, I do hope to show we can arm ourselves with lessons from history and some logical framing, which will at least help us to recognise the difference between positive and negative steps to take, when it comes to thinking about rules for international trade relationships.

In this essay, the word 'rules' refers to both the deliberate legal rules or policies constructed by governments and international organisations, and also rules in the sense of the rules of economic behaviour and consequences which can be discovered and observed. This second meaning refers to rules that the science of economics can establish or identify, which describe and try to explain human economic decisions and the relationships between economic factors. (Like the dual meaning of the word 'rules' here, the word 'laws' likewise has a similar dual meaning, as it is used to describe the 'laws of science' which have been discovered rather than created, like for example the 'laws of gravity'. And then, of course, more commonly, the word is used to describe laws which are not discovered but artificially constructed and enforced by governments.) Ascertaining both what are the scientific rules of economics applicable, or what are the best rules to be designed and implemented by governments and international organisations, are both of interest in this essay.

CHAPTER ONE

Different Examples of Rules Relating to International Trade Throughout History.

In earlier centuries, the rules and aims of trade were largely tied to power relationships between countries and nation-building.

The early history of trade is usually entangled amongst factors of military dominance and conflict, with empires, protectorates, and colonial subjugation predicting subsequent trade relations. The iconic examples of early trade, like that in the spices desired to improve European food, or the plunder of gold and silver from South America, are characterised by national military rivalries and instances of aggressive piracy sometimes condoned by home countries. A sore point for China in its long history is the way Britain and others used military force to gain preferential trade with China, in what are now called the 'unequal treaties' in China's own history, which every Chinese history student is taught. This era included, most shockingly, the Opium Wars, where the British used military force because they did not want that lucrative trade to be prevented from exporting into China. In British economic history, it is well studied that various wars and enmities were both triggered by, and affected, Britain's trade advantages, with the victory over Napoleon ushering in the long century of British advantage in dominating international trade routes. The fascinating and in parts, shocking story of the British East India Company, which led to the colonisation of all of India by a commercial company (later taken over by the British government after things got difficult), also illustrates vividly the interrelationship between trade, military might, and colonialism.

The history of the East India Company also illustrates that three hundred years ago, it was India and China who had the technology and desirable goods the world wanted to buy and copy, and were therefore wealthy. Silver and gold were draining out of Europe and settling in China and India, thanks to Europeans wanting, for example, the world-beating Chinese porcelain (traditionally, of course, called 'China' in English) and Indian Calico fabric. India and especially China on the other hand were not interested in buying any European goods. This one-sided desire for goods, and the subsequent gold and silver draining into China and India were one reason why at one point the British wanted so much to be allowed to sell opium into China, and why the early colonisation of India brought in such riches. The long story of how Britain and other European countries reversed this dynamic, combines the factors of trade, military dominance, technology transfer and then the further improvement of these and other technologies.

The earliest 'rules' of trade could be claimed, therefore to largely conform to a kind of 'might is right' rule, where whoever dominated the open seas or subjugated the colony, got to be the ones exploiting the best trade opportunities. A common pattern is the coloniser country forbidding the colonised country from taking part in the economic activities that were the most lucrative and cutting-edge for the time. For example, India, thanks partly to Britain's industrial inventions, which were definitely not shared until much later, was reduced from having some of the richest regions in the world, thanks largely to world-renowned cloth exports, to a relatively poorer colony exporting among other things, raw cotton. Like England had done to Ireland on a smaller scale with its wool industry, the colony country was encouraged to export the raw material back to Britain, where British companies did the more lucrative manufacturing processes, which increased the capabilities within the British economy, and helped to set the country on the path to development. Other rules which colonial empires liked to impose dictated that trade had to be carried out by their own companies and their own ships, and/ or that all trade had to go through, for example, London docks. Not all international trade was based on these power relationships, and of course the more untainted 'free' trade admired by economists has also played a large role, especially in more recent times. But the shaping of international trade always comes from a complex mix of power relationships, instances of competition beating technology, and organisational innovations.

The ideology underpinning the way politicians and commentators viewed these nationalistic trade policies in past times is now known as 'mercantilism'. This view of trade always had elements of seeking nationalist gain, winning advantage and national economic and military strength at its centre. The 'rules' for mercantilism were about cornering the most profitable markets and trade, maximising the gold coming back to the home country bank vaults, and exporting and trading in goods that other countries needed more than you needed anything they had to sell to you. Mercantilism is at odds with later free market and neoclassical thinking, because it sees trade as more of a zero-sum game of winning an advantage against other adversary countries. This is in contrast to free market, comparative advantage theories, which are more harmonious in outlook, pointing to an efficient specialisation and division of labour being able to benefit all countries. Mercantilist policies also often amount to supporting favoured producers and exporters at the expense of consumers and/or taxpayers, while the later free market economists base their theories on the point that the purpose of economies should be only focused on providing more goods and services to consumers, and maximising the size of an economy. So, for example, mercantilist policies of the past have directly or indirectly limited wages in order to maximise exports and minimise imports, a thread which runs through to today's China with its massive trade surplus.

One label put on mercantilists is that they have a 'fear of goods' or a fear of imports, where buying imports is viewed as a potential source of weakness for a country. In contrast, free traders believe having imports could be a positive thing, if you are able to export goods in return that your own country can make relatively more efficiently. Mathematical equations support elegant economic theories that prove how consumer utility is maximised by delegating trade policy rules to free markets and comparative advantage. Therefore, to be called a mercantilist by an economist has become an insult in modern times, to signify someone who has old-fashioned thinking, and has not been fully enlightened to understand these subtle benefits of free markets. But as Paul Tucker quipped in his book 'Global Discord', anyone in doubt as to whether mercantilism has or had its advantages, could visit the large stately homes built by those who practised mercantilism in past centuries, which are now dotted across the English countryside, and sometimes open to the public to pay to appreciate their grandeur and excess.[1]

"The liberal model views the state as necessarily predatory and the private sector as inherently rent-seeking. So, it advocates a strict separation between the state and private business. Mercantilism, by contrast, offers a corporatist vision in which the state and private business are allies and cooperate in pursuit of common objectives, such as domestic economic growth or national power." 'Straight Talk on Trade' Dani Rodrik p134

The 1930s is an era frequently referenced in relation to trade issues, and the writings of J. M. Keynes provide his understanding and opinions, from which rules can be drawn.

Rule 1: Imbalances and lack of reciprocity matter first and foremost. Keynes saw reparations and the hoarding of gold as the key early factors causing disharmony in international trade, and setting the conditions for the depression.

One cannot write an essay about trade without, of course, mentioning the infamous 1930s. This decade after the 1929 stock market crash is remembered as a period of depression and problematic international trade relations, and is often employed as a cautionary tale when protectionist policies are spoken of. Prior to the 1930s, famous British economist John Maynard Keynes had already first made his reputation by criticising the harsh reparation demands placed on Germany after WWI, which amongst other things, led indirectly to their infamous period of hyperinflation in the mid-1920s. The high reparations were one root cause of the dysfunctional international trading system in those decades, not to mention a factor in the extremist political course set upon by Germany.

The attraction of an assertive government with some very proactive and economically stimulating (Keynesian!) economic policies, including military spending of course, successfully reversed the depressed economic doom loop of austerity the German people were suffering under.

As shown in the extracts below, Keynes, with the cutting criticism he was famous for, highlighted the logical inconsistency of the situation Germany, and hence the wider world trade system, was put in after WWI, which Keynes with his Cassandra-like foresight had warned of years before. Germany was obligated to pay stiff reparations to other countries for WWI, while at the same time those other countries, even those with healthy trade surpluses like the US, were increasing their trade barriers, which prevented Germany from successfully exporting into their consumer markets. The logical inconsistency was that Germany had to export, as this was the only way for a broke country to earn the gold to pay the reparations. Especially after 1929, the major Western economies were instead all trying to out-export one another, and in many instances, putting downward pressure on their consumption and wage rates to try to win this competitive game.

This particular damaging dynamic was aided by the Gold Standard, the rules of which meant countries could be tempted to act in a way to acquire maximum gold reserves, while in the absence of such a system, exchange rate values of currencies would have floated towards an equilibrium, automatically reducing international imbalances. Within the confines of the Gold Standard system of fixed exchange rates, if a country had a trade deficit or, like Germany, needed to have a trade surplus to pay reparations, the exchange rate of its national currency would not, as now, lower through market forces or monetary policy. Without this exchange rate option, the tail had to wag the dog, and the whole national economy had to be put under recessionary pressure to lower wages and costs in order to make exports more competitive abroad and reduce the demand for imports at home. But every country doing this competitive austerity, of course, helped to spiral the Western world into the Great Depression.

For how are we to increase our exports? For Mr Simon [someone who wrote a response to one of Keynes's articles on trade] *tells us that he would have to reduce his* [Britain's] *wages by 20 per cent in order to be on level terms with Germany, and I have no doubt that he is right. Has he any prospect of doing this? If he could, does he feel sure that Germany would not reply with a further reduction of her wages, seeing that we have bound her by treaty* [reparations needed to be paid essentially from export earnings] *under dire penalties to compete successfully with ourselves (in effect), however much we reduce our wages to reduce hers by more?* Spring 1931 'Collected Works vol XX' p499.

On these will fall the curse of Midas. As a result of their unwillingness to exchange their exports except for gold their export trade will dry up and disappear until they no longer have either a favourable trade balance or foreign deposits to repatriate. This means in the main France and the United States. Their loss of export trade will be an inevitable, a predictable, outcome of their own actions. These countries, largely for reasons resulting from the war [WW1] *and the war settlements, are owed much money by* *the rest of the world. They erect tariff barriers which prevent payment of these sums in goods. They are unwilling to lend it. They have already taken nearly all the available surplus gold in the whole world. There remained, in logic, only one way by which the rest of the world could maintain its solvency and self-respect; namely, to cease purchasing these countries' exports. So long as the gold standard is preserved—which means that the prices of international commodities must be much the same everywhere—this involved a competitive campaign of deflation, each of us trying to get our prices down faster than the others, a campaign which had intensified unemployment and business losses to an unendurable pitch.* September 1931 'The End of the Gold Standard', Essays in Persuasion, 'Collected Works vol IV' p248*

The whole world is heartily sick of the selfishness and folly with which the international gold standard is being worked. Instead of being a means of facilitating international trade, the gold standard has become a curse laid upon the economic life of the world. ... It is only necessary to look at the present distribution of the world's gold supplies. Half the world's gold stocks are now held by America. ... At the present time the American gold stock is about £1,000,000,000 and the French £471,000,000. The reason for this concentration of gold in America and France is that these countries have not lent their surplus balance on international account as Great Britain used to do in the past. France appears to have employed virtually the whole of her international surplus during the last three or four years in the purchase of gold and short-term liquid claims instead of embarking on long-term investments abroad. The attitude towards long-term investments of investors in the United States has varied but has been generally unfavourable, ... It was the opinion of the Macmillan Committee that the disposition of these creditor countries to employ their international balances in the purchase of liquid claims, including gold, had been primarily responsible for the disastrous fall in the level of world prices. Yet it is one of the objects of the gold standard to maintain stability of the international price level. Autumn 1931 'Collected Works vol XX' p600

Of course, Keynes was a proud Brit and did tend to adjust his arguments to fit British interests and pride on occasion. However, it is interesting that he notes above that he believes that the US and France were harming the world economy by wanting to keep gold in return for their trade surpluses, rather than lend out capital for investment in developing countries, thus recirculating demand, as he claims Britain did when it had trade surpluses in earlier decades. One example he gives is Britain providing the capital for loans to Argentina, so it could build railways and buy British-made steam trains to help grow its economy, with part of this growth and loan repayment, for example, coming from selling Argentine beef products back to Britain. Keynes argues that hoarding gold, rather than recirculating the cash from trade surpluses into stimulating foreign business investments, was sucking what he would later call aggregate demand out of the world economy. It was the lived experience of going through the competitive austerity, escalating tariffs, and the recognition of the logical inconsistencies which Keynes and others were pointing out, which led to the search for the creation of better rules, mechanisms and organisations to manage international trade after WWII.

Rule 2: Tariffs were more a symptom than a cause of the Great Depression. For Keynes, the issue was low aggregate demand and policies of competitive austerity within and between nations, of which tariffs were just a tool, aggressive if they perpetuated trade surpluses, but self-defence if enacted by a deficit country.

An important distinction that is often missed in the knee-jerk use of the 1930s as an example of the dangers of protectionism and tariffs, is that, as Keynes did more than anyone to explain above, it was countries going too far in competing with each other to increase their trade surpluses that was at the root of the harm. The infamous 1930s tariffs were the policy tools that were sometimes used aggressively to perpetuate those trade surpluses. But equally as often as with Britain at one point, tariffs were used defensively as a last resort to try to correct the legitimate difficulty trade deficits were causing within the Gold Standard system, where changing exchange rates was not an easy option.

The arguments of the most ill-informed free traders often summarise the 1930s world trade situation as being that first, tariffs were increased, then trade reduced, then growth reduced turning a recession into a worldwide depression. A more accurate summary would start with the distortions caused by some countries wishing to maintain a trade surplus, and with the help of the Gold Standard, build up their gold reserves, while into this mix Germany was also being 'held by treaty' to need a trade surplus to earn the gold to pay its reparations. The 1929 stock market crash then introduced negative sentiments, and with hindsight, the monetary responses of the authorities in the US let the volume of money in their economy fall too far, as everyone repaid debts, absorbed losses and tightened their belts. This and similar policies in other countries introduced a spiral of austerity and deflationary conditions. In terms of trade, governments were tempted to use protection to improve their own sagging domestic demand at the expense of demand in other countries. The temptation was that protection would create prosperity for a country's industries and workers by winning export business and increasing home-produced goods. The weakness in this thinking is that trading partners do not want to accept a negative relationship, and so they retaliate. Tariffs were the weapons in these trade conflicts, and indeed their escalation made things worse. But the original sin was the disharmony of countries having selfish trade objectives which were incompatible with each other, mixed with, and attempted to be aided by, deflation and austerity. The issue is that winning trade from trade partners is a zero-sum game at best when looked at from the international level. While austerity policies or sentiments in an economy causing low business confidence, and also deflationary monetary conditions pushing down on demand, is a negative drag, pulling down total world demand. A zero-sum effect added to a negative effect is still a negative effect overall, hence the Great Depression.

Tariffs do lead to reduced efficiency and a dead loss to the world economy, if things are not produced in the countries that can produce them the most efficiently. But this kind of loss of efficiency would amount to small percentages, while the depression saw much greater drops in GDP. To map the history of tariff levels and countries' growth rates does not support the argument that tariffs themselves caused all the damage of the depression. Note the US throughout most of the 19th century, or Japan in the 1960s and 70s, or South Korea in the 1970s and 80s, with high tariffs and high growth.

"At the time of Smoot-Hawley we ran an unreasonable trade surplus that we wished to maintain. We now run a damaging deficit that the whole world knows we must correct." Warren Buffett 2003 (see Chapter Five)

Below, Keynes, writing in 1932 about the upcoming World Economic Conference, highlighted that he thought tariffs were a symptom of the other factors that were causing the depression, and not the primary cause. For Keynes, tariffs were the short-sighted policies governments without deficits were using to try to increase demand for their own goods at the expense of other countries. This attempt at stimulating domestic industry by protection was for Keynes the less desirable alternative to what they should have been doing, which was all governments doing more to increase demand generally, which is the policy impetus which Keynes' name is still most associated with. In Keynes' opinion, tariffs were a tool which were needed by Britain in an emergency to protect the country from a trade deficit and unsustainable financial pressures. A generalisation or rule could therefore be made from Keynes' writing, that he believed tariffs as a last resort to reduce a trade deficit were excusable, but tariffs to act as economic stimulus for the industry of one's own country at the expense of other countries, when you don't have a trade deficit, is acting in bad faith and against the common good. He believed that what are now called 'Keynesian' (fiscal) and other stimulus policies such as monetary policies should be used to increase domestic aggregate demand in times of recession, and not protectionist policies, which were trying to borrow the demand of consumers in other countries. 'Beggar thy neighbour' is the famous phrase often used in relation to tariffs in this era, to illustrate how using tariffs to grab economic demand from abroad in times of recession was in bad faith and fundamentally not effective in the long term as trade partners usually retaliate.

The latest extravagances of tariffs and quotas, exchange restrictions, the default of debts, the collapse of the gold standard, even the fall of prices itself, are mainly symptoms. No one has desired these things; none of them is the expression of deliberate policy; they have been forced upon us as the expression and the result of more fundamental forces. It is as though a council of doctors, summoned to cure colds in the head, were to pass resolutions that it is desirable to stop sniffling and that a man who coughs is a nuisance to his neighbours. ... There is one, and only one, genuine remedy; namely, to increase demand—in other words to increase expenditure. ... If we all begin purchasing again, we shall all have the means to do so. The appropriate stimulus to the activity of trade will vary from nation to nation; in some a relief from taxation, in some a program of public works, in some an expansion of credit, in some a relaxation of exchange and import restrictions, in some a repayment of pressing debts, in some the mere removal of anxieties and fear, in some the mere stimulus to the lords of business to be courageous and active again. 'Collected Works vol XXI' p212, 213, 215.

Rule 3: Tariffs are sometimes justified if your aims match improving international equilibrium. Keynes for a while saw using tariffs as a way to address Britain's difficult trade deficit crisis, in preference to leaving the Gold Standard and devaluing, as that had implications for financial markets.

A few years before, Britain was experiencing a crisis in its international flows of money in the City of London. The Bank of England had kept British interest rates very high for a few years by this point, in order to prevent too much lending to other countries, made attractive by the overvalued Pound. But the high interest rates, as always, were also a dampener on domestic industry and the economy in general, making foreign investment still more attractive in comparison. The impetus to lend abroad was incompatible with Britain's trade deficit because as always, the currency exchange and trade identity meant the value of money being invested abroad on net could only be as large as the value to which exports were greater than imports on net. Keynes strongly supported Britain adopting tariffs to get through the difficult period, and below suggests it would give Britain 'breathing space' to sort things out.

In Keynes' writing, there is always a keen eye for the identities and magnitudes of the practical values and flows of money involved in economics. In his writing the magnitudes and identities are often used to illustrate situations of disequilibrium, where the implicit point is that policies and actions that move things towards a better balance or equilibrium are a positive step. To the eyes of a modern person with some economic knowledge, the issue of the overvalued and fixed exchange rate of the Gold Standard was the central culprit of the disequilibrium in Britain at that time, and even before 1929. But Keynes was at first reluctant to leave the Gold Standard exchange system, because of the Pound Sterling's and the financial centre of the City of London's role and implicit obligations in world finance, much like the Dollar and New York today. Also, London had a position as a large creditor to the rest of the world, meaning the large interest payments coming back every year would be hit by a devaluation. Devaluation was also deemed to be bad for financial market confidence, stability, and London's prestige. So with devaluation off the Gold Standard fix not deemed desirable, Keynes judged that tariffs were the next best option, as he explains below.

I have reached my own conclusions as the result of continuous reflection over many months, without enthusiasm, and as the result of the gradual elimination of the practicable alternatives as being even more undesirable. Nor do I suppose for one moment that a revenue tariff by itself will see us out of our troubles. Indeed, I mainly support it because it will give us a margin of resources and a breathing space, undercover of which we can do other things. 'Collected Works vol XX' p498

1. My proposal is for a uniform tariff of, say, 10 per cent on all imports whatsoever, including food, and a bounty of the same amount on all exports whatsoever.

2. The effect of such an arrangement on international trade would be to restore the conditions which would exist under free trade if money costs were reduced 10 per cent.

3. It has, in effect, the same result as devaluation, except that it leaves sterling's international obligations unchanged in terms of gold. There are, obviously, very great advantages in this from the point of view of national credit. Moreover, since we are a creditor nation in terms of sterling and our imports exceed our exports, there is actually a pecuniary benefit to us in leaving the gold value of sterling alone.

12. The system would be capable of being adjusted from time to time with the changing value of money. Indeed, it might be laid down from the outset that the rate of the tariff-bounty would be annually increased or decreased according to the international price level. Thus, if international prices were to fall another 5 per cent the tariff-bounty could be increased 5 per cent. On the other hand, if they rise by an adequate amount, it could be abolished. Indeed, it is a method of rendering us to some extent independent of external instability in the value of money without interfering with the position of London as an international financial centre and as a depository of short-loan funds. Indeed, the tendency to increase tariffs everywhere in the last few years may be interpreted as an instinctive act of self-protection against the instability of the external value of gold. Unless some way can be found of making money wages habitually mobile, it is difficult to see how we can do without such a device in the event of the world value of gold being highly fluctuating.

13. It would not help if every other country followed suit. But this is equally true of a reduction of money wages. 'Collected Works vol XX' p416-8

(a) Devaluation

Theoretically, the most obvious and comprehensive method of effecting the desired object would be to leave money incomes alone but to change the monetary standard, e.g., by diminishing by 10 per cent the gold parity of sterling. This would have the advantage of bringing the direct, initial benefit to those industries which need it most, mainly, to the foreign-trade industries. It would involve no interference with contract, since debts are legally fixed in terms of sterling and not in terms of gold. It would affect every class of income without the necessity of any other special measures. For a country which was not an international banker and was not owed large sums from abroad fixed in terms of sterling, this would be the simplest solution. We have already agreed, however, that for a country in the special circumstances of Great Britain, the disadvantages would greatly outweigh the advantages, and we have concurred with our colleagues in rejecting it.

(b) Tariffs plus Bounties

Precisely the same effect as those produced by devaluation of sterling by a given percentage could be brought about by a tariff of the same percentage on all imports together with an equal subsidy on all exports, except that this measure would leave sterling international obligations unchanged in terms of gold. This proposal would avoid the injury to the national credit and to our receipts from foreign loans fixed in terms of sterling which would ensue on devaluation. ...
'Collected Works vol XX' p295-6.

Once financial pressures made it inevitable that Britain would come off the Gold Standard exchange system, Keynes felt it was a good thing. Keynes felt that the implicit obligations and interests of the City of London financial and banking system had been defended as much as possible, but that devaluation was eventually inevitable. The reduced exchange rate of the Pound then meant the tariff policies were now less needed, as he argues below. I believe it is possible to see in Keynes' writing, a distinction between using tariffs to cure a disequilibrium in trade and financial flows between countries, and using tariffs in a way in which would make a disequilibrium between countries worse. The first is self-defence, the latter is aggressive.

Until recently I was urging on Liberals and others the importance of accepting a general tariff as a means of mitigating the effects of the obvious disequilibrium between money-costs at home and abroad. But the events of the last week have made a great difference. ... In these circumstances we cannot continue as if nothing had happened. It is impossible to have a rational discussion about tariffs so long as the currency question is altogether unsolved. For until we know more about the probable future level of sterling in relation to gold and, above all, until we know how many other countries are going to follow our example, it is impossible to say what our competitive position is going to be.

May I urge that the immediate question for attention is not a tariff but the currency question? It is the latter which is urgent and important. ... Meanwhile, proposals for high protection have ceased to be urgent. To throw the country into turmoil over them to the neglect of this other more urgent and important problem would be a wrong and foolish thing. Let us give our whole attention and our united energies to devising a sound international currency policy for ourselves and the rest of the world. For it is futile to suppose that we can recover our formal prosperity without such a policy, or that tariffs can be any substitute for it. When the currency question has been settled, then we can return to protection and our other domestic issues with a solid basis to go upon; and that will be the time for a General Election. Letter to The Times, Sep 1931, 'Collected Works vol IX' Essays in Persuasion p243

Rule 4: Throughout Keynes' writing on tariffs and protection, he always warned of their pitfalls and dangers. He also noted the often contradictory and insincere motivations and justifications put forward for using them.

From the start, Keynes always emphasised the problems and pitfalls of tariffs, and the problematic and insincere justifications of some of those who support them. But Keynes had a very interventionist frame of mind and was at certain periods very practically involved in Britain's very real international finance issues and crises, where idealism often had to take a back seat. In the final extract below, Keynes notes the inconsistency very relevant today, of using tariffs both as an instantly adjustable negotiating or retaliation tool, but then also as a basis for support for domestic industry where predictability is important.

The path of wisdom in these matters is, then, a narrow one, to be trodden safely only by those who see the pitfalls on both sides. Neither free trade nor protection can present a theoretical case which entitles it to claim supremacy in practice. Protection is a dangerous and expensive method of redressing a want of balance and security in a nation's economic life. But there are times when we cannot safely trust ourselves to the blindness of economic forces; and when no alternative weapon as efficacious as tariffs lies ready to our hand. The Listener, 30 November 1932. 'Collected Works vol XXI' p210

The complication of the free trade issue has generally arisen in the past from the fact that whilst protectionists have really wanted protection for its own fallacious sake, they have generally advanced under a thick smoke-screen of the exceptional cases—agriculture and race-virility, key industries, infant industries, dumping, preference, retaliation, and making the foreigner pay. ... There remains retaliation available for an occasional mention. But the worst of this cry is its utter inconsistency with the main cry of providing permanent employment. For it is of the essence of retaliation that the duties are put on with the idea of taking them off again, soon and suddenly, when they have served their purpose. It is obvious that no expansion of home industry could be started under the precarious and deceptive shelter of retaliatory duties. 'Collected Works vol XIX' p150-1

Game Theory type thinking can help to explain why free trade rules are at the same time both desirable, and yet need agreements and negotiations to make countries follow the rules.

To a non-economist, a natural question that would spring to mind regarding free trade would be: "if free trade is so desirable and great, why do countries have to be forced and cajoled through the negotiation of trade agreements and WTO 'rounds' to do it and stick to it?" Game theory-type thinking is the best way to explain this inconsistency. Two things can both be true at the same time. Yes, in most circumstances leaving the location of the production of goods and services to be dictated by free market forces and free trade will settle on the most efficient division of labour and maximise world consumption and growth in theoretical terms. But the game theory dynamic present, also means it is true that if the rest of the world is complying with this efficient division of labour and maximising consumption and growth, it can be possible to design industrial and protectionist policies for your own country to give your own domestic producers an advantage in desirable sectors and proactively shape your own future production specialisms and clusters.

In this way of thinking, free trade is the best outcome to grow the world economic cake, but for individual countries or 'players', it can be only the second-best outcome. If one participating country strays from these rules of free trade by using subsidies, tariffs, and other industrial policies, then if they get the policies right, this could represent their country going from the second-best to the best option for themselves. The 'cheating' country is shaping its future by aggressively controlling which affluent economic activities it is going to produce in the future, while the rest of the players remain in the passive stance of dutifully letting their consumers choose which goods and services to buy, based only on things most consumers care about, like prices and value for money, which could of course mean imports.

But as is typical in the iconic game theory games, the cheating of an individual player only pays off as long as the other players are not also cheating. The passive players, now seeing that the proactive or cheating country has abandoned the mutual common-good understanding, are then themselves motivated to also move towards proactive, targeted industrial and protectionist policies to defend and improve the position of their domestic producers. Through countries breaking ranks from their second-best, common-good option, they are now all in danger of ending up with their third-best option for everyone, where they are all proactively trying to dominate desirable sectors of production and all using a web of tariffs and subsidies to try to improve their domestic position. This leads to goods and services no longer being produced under neat and efficient free trade and free market rules, where they can be produced most efficiently. Instead, taken to extreme, now there are no 'rules' as such, except the arbitrary political will of different governments regarding how far to go to subsidise and protect, with all the accompanying risk of political capture, complacency and even corruption that might entail. The neat rules of free trade and comparative advantage are replaced by a chaotic absence of rules.

This third-best option can logically lead to a greater number of smaller and less efficient producers, where there is less competitive pressure for producers to innovate and compete, and smaller production volumes as the natural tendency of capitalism to concentrate and gain efficiencies and economies of scale has been thwarted. This understanding of free trade versus industrial and protectionist policies describes quite well the way international treaties and trade rounds can create and encourage 'common good' restraining behaviour, which increases GDP. It also explains why in times of unfavourable economic conditions like the 1930s, the instance of protectionism goes up, as successive countries felt the political pressure of economic depression at home, including high unemployment, and sacrificed the general common good understandings. But as game theory predicts, when everyone started 'cheating', so the rewards for cheating went down, and the costs to the world economy of the duplication and the less efficient division of labour reduced the size of the whole economic cake. This way of thinking, of course, justifies the need for an effective institution like the World Trade Organization, promoting the general good and preventing a race to the bottom of retaliatory cheating. This game theory way of thinking fits quite well with the fragility and incompleteness of free trade behaviour throughout history, and the way it takes effort for countries to create mutual agreements to try to maintain a desirable common good outcome for all.

"Trade pacts arise so that all can bind themselves to the mast of not embarking on the inferior-equilibrium course." 'Global Discord' Paul Tucker p412

The Bretton Woods rules, structures, and institutions, sought to create a bias towards more trade, and more support to help countries with crises in trade and other international financial flows.

Towards the end of WWII, there was the famous Bretton Woods conference at the large US resort hotel in the place of that name. Here, government delegations made up of officials and economists from many countries came together to design and agree upon the organisations, rules and architecture of the post-war international financial and trading systems. The Americans dominated the negotiations, in no small part because the British, French and other Europeans, were dependent on US loans and arms supplies, and the US funds and financial might would obviously underwrite any new international systems. But although the Americans dominated proceedings, and although his pet solution of a special international currency did not gain acceptance, the intellectual godfather of the Bretton Woods conference was the British lead representative, Keynes. His writing from the last two decades had proven prescient on many matters, and his main analysis regarding the problems and a better way forward for international economic relations, had gained a wider consensus among economists and politicians of many countries, and most importantly, the support of US government officials.

One of Keynes' key influences on the Bretton Woods conference, was the belief that the world trade and financial system should contain mechanisms that could provide emergency credit to countries experiencing difficulties. This could provide a bias towards economic stimulus and growth, and prevent a return to the downward spirals of lowering export prices, competitive national austerity policies to increase exports and reduce imports, and competitive devaluing of currencies. The aim was to prevent a repeat of the 1930s escalating 'beggar thy neighbour' defensive tariffs aimed at attempting to force manufacturing jobs back to your own country. The ideal was for the economies of the world to be able, through conducive conditions, to grow, with the new concepts of gross domestic product and a new Keynesian understanding of multiplier effects creating new economic hopes that all countries could grow, and that the growth of other countries was a benefit to one's own country due to trading opportunities, and not a threat as in the older mercantilist mindset.

Dear [Harry] White,

In accordance with my undertaking last Saturday, I now enclose an initialled copy of the Draft Directive and of the Minutes as they emerged from our final conversation on Saturday. ...

Anglo-American Draft Statement of Principles

Joint statement by experts of united and associated nations on the establishment of an international stabilisation fund

I. Preamble

The International Stabilisation Fund is designed as a permanent institution for international monetary cooperation. The Fund is intended to facilitate the balanced growth of international trade and to contribute in this way to the maintenance of a high level of employment. The Fund is expected to provide the machinery for consultation on international monetary problems. The resources of the Fund are to be available under adequate safeguards to help member countries to maintain currency stability while giving them time to correct maladjustments in their balance of payments without resorting to extreme measures destructive to international prosperity. Keynes Oct 1943 'Collected Works vol XXV' p379-80.

As well as the new GDP and Keynesian multiplier theories, the development in economics of theories that showed the benefits of trade were being advanced at this time. These trade theories are called by some the 'crown jewels' of economics. This is because in a subject like economics, which is full of subjectivity and grey areas, and theories that can be reasonably disputed, the body of work proving the benefits of free trade and comparative advantage is elegant, able to be mathematically demonstrated, rational, and hard to dispute. (To someone interested but not having studied economics, a search online for 'understanding comparative advantage theories' might be informative.)

In summary, comparative advantage theories explain how trade can be a positive-sum game, meaning that with the same labour and other inputs, specialising and trading can increase the goods available for both trading countries to consume. The main efficiency gains of trade for a developed country come from the way free markets search out, select and encourage specialisms which enable the companies and workers of that country to leverage the areas where they are most efficient. For example, if a rich country is efficient at making cars, it can use its workers on high wages to help build a car for 40 hours a week. If it trades that car with a developing country, the favourable relative prices and relative wages mean that the equivalent of that 40 hours of labour contributing to a car, is exchanged for goods that contain far more hours of labour, like, for example, 200 hours of labour contributing to producing clothes. So the trade has leveraged up the potential for man/woman labour hours of goods able to be consumed by the developed country to far more than would be possible if there was no trade and all labour-intensive goods were produced domestically. In other words, trade can be an effective device for a country to create more consumption with the same inputs and resources.

It is better to employ our capital and our labour in trades where we are relatively more efficient than other people are and to exchange the products of these trades for goods in the production of which we are relatively less efficient. Every sane man pursues this principle in his private life. He concentrates his energies on those employments where his efficiency is greatest in comparison with other people's; and leaves to others what they can do better than he can. Keynes 'Collected Works vol XIX' p147

One of Keynes' key observations was that in the previous decades, when an imbalance of trade came about, the country in a trade deficit position was under heavy pressure to reduce their deficit, including by tariffs and the austerity-causing means mentioned above, like holding down wage rates and consumption. But a country with a trade surplus was under no such pressure to reduce their surplus, even though in a closed system, the surpluses were just as much of a culprit of the imbalance as the deficits. As Keynes was claiming in the extracts in the previous section, the trade surplus countries often acted in ways to prolong the imbalance, rather than return to a more balanced equilibrium situation. In the end, although the Americans succeeded in achieving structures in which the US dollar was central, they also agreed to create the International Monetary Fund, which was focused on providing easy loans to countries that were experiencing currency exchange and trade deficit issues. The thinking was that if there were no countries in the position in which Germany had been in the 1920s and early 1930s, under pressure to export at any price, then there would be less likelihood of significant downward pressure on the prices in the wider trading system, and less incentive to want to employ self-protecting tariffs. The World Bank and the International Monetary Fund would help to maintain a proactively expansionary bias in the world economy, which could support those experiencing recessionary pressures, deficit issues, and financial crises, rather than the rest of the world fearing their desperate, cheap exports. The later Marshall Plan of generous aid and finance from the US to Europe and Japan, also continued the theme of pro-stimulus and pro-trade policies, trying to keep the world economy buoyant and money circulating to where it could be employed most productively.

Then a very fundamental point: where there is a want of balance in trade dealings so that the imports of some countries are much greater than their exports and the exports of other countries much greater than their imports, when that happens, and it may happen for perfectly good reasons, the pressure of adjustment should not fall, as it has in the past, almost wholly on the weaker country, the debtor. The creditor may be equally to blame, he may be less to blame, he may also be more to blame. We should like to have a set-up which made it as much the duty of the creditor country as of the debtor country to ensure a proper balance. If he can just insist on gold, which perhaps the debtor has not got, he makes the only alternative the pressure of deflation and contraction of trade so as to get an export equilibrium on a lower basis. If we could have a system which would put pressure on the creditor as much as the debtor, we might be a great step forward to removing the other consequential difficulties of want of balance. And along with that, there should be, we think, an atmosphere of expansion rather than the contrary. We should look forward to world trade being much greater than it has been in the past, to the wealth of the world being much greater, the scale of things being larger, and there should not be some pressure on all of us, some contractionist feeling, some elemental feature of the system which was forcing us in our own short-sighted policy to contract rather than expand. Keynes, speech to a meeting of European Allies, Feb 1943 'Collected Works vol XXV' p208

Thinking about trade in terms of game theory concepts is arguably a good basis from which to approach the role and objectives of the World Trade Organization, (which was formerly before 1994 the General Agreement on Tariffs and

Trade). The intention of the GATT was to have an international body to encourage countries to have lower trade barriers and to increase trade. In theoretical terms, this would bring countries closer towards an ideal situation, where trade flows were dictated by economic efficiency and comparative advantage, producing an efficiency dividend for all countries to share. The GATT also reflected a desire that trade be arranged along more progressive and equal lines, where less powerful countries had a more level playing field and an organisation to stick up for their trade interests against more powerful countries. This represented trying to leave behind trade relationships based on colonialism, military power and other 'might is right' patterns. The WTO, therefore aspires to represent the triumph of free market economic theory and rules-based, common-good goals. But it is also worth noting that although the WTO gains a great deal of legitimacy from high-minded economic principles, critics can also note instances where large companies have successfully lobbied the most powerful rich-country governments to include components of WTO trade agreements for commercial rather than idealist motives.

When the GATT transformed into the WTO in 1994, a main difference was that the WTO was given the added dimension of the means and structures to enforce sanctions against countries it deemed as refusing to respond to its rules and judgments. The structure of the Appellate Body was created, made up of judges to judge disputes, and a history of case law began to be built up, available to be applied to subsequent disputes. The WTO can theoretically, therefore more forcefully act as a referee between countries, pushing back against any self-interested behaviour, which means, in theory every country can feel the benefit from the greater collective restraint and greater common good outcomes. The advent of the WTO's sanctioning powers meant individual countries were encouraged to settle their disputes and attempt to get satisfaction through the WTO, rather than using the traditional routes of their own unilateral trade sanctions and threats.

The WTO has many important rules that reflect its central aspiration to improve and increase world trade. The 'Most Favoured Nation' (MFN) concept is a key one, where member countries are pressured to have trade barriers like tariffs with all other member countries, which are equally as good or as low as any terms they agree with any other individual member country. So, this means countries are pressured away from having preferential relations with favoured partners, but are encouraged to offer every member the best terms and concessions agreed with any one country. It effectively enacts a bias or ratchet effect towards more free trade and fewer trade barriers and restrictions, which matches the core values and aims of the WTO. In general, tariffs between major developed countries have gone down substantially since the GATT and WTO have been in place, and economists argue this has played a large role in making the world richer.

Other interesting areas of WTO rules highlight more subtly the economic concepts of comparative advantage that support free trade theories and maximise economic utility. In investigating trade disputes, for example, the WTO would be keen to ascertain the true commercial competitiveness of a country's domestic producers in a particular market and to draw careful lines between level playing field competition, and perceived unfair advantages like government subsidies.

WTO investigations and judgements reflect a certain concept of what a level playing field in trading should be, with certain competitive advantages being acceptable within the rules, and certain advantages unacceptable. For a country to have a competitive advantage due to having a generally lower wage rate is acceptable, and the basis for a large amount of the shifting patterns of international trade in recent decades. The comparative advantage theory can justify a country with abundant, low-paid labour and scarce capital per worker, specialising in, for example, labour-intensive clothing sectors. If a country has built up economies of scale and specialist knowledge and skills within a sector, it is also fine that this country should dominate the market of these sectors. These are perceived as legitimate advantages that aid a country's competitiveness. But if the advantages a country's producers have are based on government subsidies or other types of government assistance, this is perceived as not legitimate, but as interfering with free trade principles.

The perception of what are legitimate competitive advantages to motivate trade is a contentious area. What if, like China, low wage rates are not just representing the level of economic development, but reflecting a lower share than normal going to labour versus the owners of capital and government? And then there are other contentious issues that can give developing countries advantages that win them trade, such as using child labour in the footwear and clothing sectors, lack of worker rights and banning of unionisation, lower environmental standards, and hazardous working conditions. These kinds of issues fuel and legitimise concerns over trading with developing countries and globalisation in general. But those who want to maintain a free trading system warn that these legitimate issues can be used as an excuse for old-fashioned protectionism by those who wanted the protectionism anyway.[2]

The concept of 'dumping', meaning exporting goods at a price deemed to be below that charged in the exporter's domestic market, is an important area of trade disputes within the WTO system. Anti-dumping duties are a very common protection tool used by countries trying to protect their domestic producers. Part of China's accession to the WTO in 2001 included a clause that China was to be deemed a 'Non-Market Economy' for purposes of WTO rules and technicalities for fifteen years after accession. Although China protests otherwise, the US and others still classify China as an NME for WTO dumping dispute purposes. This allows complainant countries to assume the costs or prices of goods in other, more free-market countries with a similar wage rate, as a guide or proxy for the assumed true cost or prices in China, and therefore as a starting point for the calculations in a dispute claiming 'dumping' of goods. This assertion reveals a lot about the rules and theory underpinning the WTO's approach. According to neoclassical economic theory, in a free-market economy, the 'prices' of goods and services, and the prices of their inputs at every stage are viewed as centrally important information. It is all these prices that are the basis for the workings of the whole complex structure of self-interested decision-making, within the free market system. Adam Smith's famous invisible hand needs, more than anything, accurate prices to do its job properly, and incorrect prices mean incorrect allocation decisions are made. The efficiency benefits of following free market systems depend entirely on the legitimacy of having correct prices to reflect the 'true' costs embodied within them, so that maximum efficient allocation results. Therefore, this is why if prices are deemed to be not legitimate due to distortions in input prices generated by government subsidies etc., then the WTO rules surrounding allegations of 'dumping' allow for proxy prices to be substituted from another economy, where there are fewer distortions.

Also, in the contentious area of China's 'State Owned Enterprises' (SOEs) (discussed further later), an important factor in disputes is ascertaining when they are, or are not, acting in a way that shows pure commercial self-interest. The implicit point is that evidence that they are departing from commercial self-interest is a sign of government influence, and therefore a sign that they are acting as 'public bodies' rather than commercial businesses.[3] The series of logical steps made in asserting the value of free markets, level playing field competition, and decision structures responding only to true prices and profits leads to this interesting situation. Any diversions from complete financial selfishness by SOEs become a possible sign of guilt, in terms of evidence of unfair government subsidy or influence potentially being in play. In this topsy-turvy game, the rules are that to be commercially selfish is to be innocently playing the game properly, while acting under the influence of other factors and not maximising selfish behaviour, or giving goods or services too generously to one's trading partners, is deemed as suspicious.

The decades after WWII for the West saw high growth rates, lowering trade barriers and improving affluence. The influence of the policies and institutions begun at Bretton Woods set the tone for a trade-friendly international environment, but the free market fundamentalism and hyper-globalization of more recent decades had yet to arrive. The damaging competitive austerity policies of the 1930s had been banished, while things which helped nation states get strong, like capital controls and infant industry protectionist policies were not yet so frowned upon as they were to be later.

Alternative economists believe the rules of free trade ideology focus only on present economic capabilities, and neglect how countries have always used industrial policies to develop their economies.

Free trade theories and rules suggest the most efficient way to organise any economy, and indeed the world economy. As discussed above, therefore there is fundamental truth in the premise of the WTO's remit, that more free trade can increase global prosperity, and that competitive and retaliatory industrial and protectionist policies reduce the size of the global economic pie. This is the free market and free trade case. But one weakness in this approach is that this efficiency is based only on 'present' capabilities and prices, as prices supposedly represent true relative costs in order to make the system maximise efficient allocation. The reality of economic history also shows again and again that producing or making certain goods and services leads to different outcomes, and countries have progressed by targeting or aspiring to certain economic activities, which free trade alone would never encourage them to pursue. Thus, the perennial debate between free market trade and employing industrial policy was never really settled, and industrial and protectionist policies are becoming ever more prominent in present times.

*"For fear of empowering the "protectionist barbarian's",
trade economists have been prone to exaggerate the benefits
of trade and downplay its distributional and other costs. ...
A far better strategy for economists is to be open about the
ambiguity and context-specificity of most results in
economics—to flaunt the diversity rather than hide it. "*
'Straight Talk on Trade' Dani Rodrik p138

The free market and free trade ideals can ignore and neglect
a wealth of knowledge and practical history concerning how
virtually all developed countries used industrial and
protectionist policies to kickstart sectors of production they
wanted to become capable and efficient in. This competing
ideology rejects the wisdom of letting market demand alone
dictate what your country produces and instead focuses on
governments being deliberate in the building up of
capabilities and knowledge and the generation of spill-overs
and clusters of expertise. The ideas supporting infant
industry and industrial policies are very old, and German
economist Friedrich List in the 19th century was one of the
first economists to popularise them. He argued that free
trade was good for a country that already had desirable
sectors of economic activity, but government intervention
was necessary for those countries that did not have them,
and wanted to nurture world-competitive companies with
more desirable economic competencies.

*"Any nation which, by means of protective duties and
restrictions on navigation, has raised her manufacturing
power and her navigation to such a degree of development
that no other nation can sustain free competition with her,
can do nothing wiser than to throw away these ladders of
her greatness, to preach to other nations the benefits of free*

trade, and to declare in penitent tones that she has hitherto wandered in the paths of error, and has now for the first time succeeded in discovering the truth." 'The National System of Political Economy' Friedrich List.

A key weakness of free trade theory, and the foundation on which industrial policy arguments rest, is that history shows partaking in different economic activities has fundamentally different outcomes for a country's development prospects. Alternative or heterodox economists who have made these arguments, such as Erik Reinert and Ha-Joon Chang, present a wealth of history and practical examples of where a country's industrial policies helped it to develop economically. Importantly in today's world, industrial policy arguments and theories can accurately explain China's impressive economic growth, while in contrast, China breaks in quite extreme ways, many of the tenets of free market theories of economic development. The industrial policy school arguments assert that different goods and services go through specific periods of productivity gains and innovations, and to be a country or region, or even just a city, with a specialism in certain sectors while they are experiencing these productivity booms, is a great boost. This is because the productivity gains and/or consumer appeal of the goods produced allow for high margins for the producing companies, allowing higher profits and investment. The higher margins also allow higher wages, sometimes allowing unionisation to force these wages higher without crippling the company, as the company can pass on the costs because it is not under the normal intense competitive pressure. Likewise for the same reasons, higher margins allow higher taxes, which allow the government to build better infrastructure and redistribute some of the gains.

"it is the interventionists who have succeeded in economic history, where it really matters." 'Straight Talk on Trade' Dani Rodrik' p133

As Erik Reinert notes, the best American business schools teach that the most profitable businesses are those that manage to carve out a business model that is not exposed to intense price competition.[4] This points to why innovative sectors can be lucrative for a country, while free market theories miss these qualitative factors and treat all economic activities as the same, and all businesses as exposed to the minimum returns of perfect competition. The industrial policy school of thought emphasises the path dependency of a country's economic capabilities, which can benefit from government intervention to help it along a more prosperous path. Achieving competency in sectors like high-end manufacturing spurs wider economic affluence, where economies of scale and mechanisation can put a country in a sweet spot, where it can have rising wages, while products are still getting cheaper, and profits are getting higher, all at the same time. Strong and persistent economic growth into a developed, rich economy, has nearly always been accompanied by a country exporting manufactured goods of ever greater complexity, with the country on this path being able to absorb relatively unskilled labour, often in the past uneducated agricultural workers, into manufacturing jobs where they increase their earnings and productivity.[5]

"The toolbox of standard textbook economics does not contain tools to record the fact that at any time there are only a few industries behaving as shoe production did at the end of the 1800s, as the car production did seventy-five

years later, and as the production of mobile phones does now." 'How the Rich got Rich ...' Erik Reinert p139

"Thus, when the world economy was conceived as a system where everybody exchanged undefined 'labour hours' without technology, without economies of scale and without synergy effects – work that everybody mastered in the same way – the path was cleared for the view that free trade could be considered beneficial to all." 'How the Rich got Rich ...' Erik Reinert p122

In contrast, the free market school of thought would focus instead only on the benefits to consumers of any productivity gains, reflecting that they have no tools in their toolbox to recognise that the special sweet spot of companies enjoying productivity gains and innovations could even exist. This is because in their model, the pervasiveness of theoretical 'perfect competition' conditions means being cutting edge, like Apple, for example, is no more profitable than any other company. Free market ideology would simply assume that any productivity gains or innovation benefits are simply passed on to consumers through competition, and not emphasise the special advantages of one sector being more desirable to be a producer in than any other. In their thinking, the market competes away high profits and the benefits from innovation straight away.

One key implication for the choice between the two approaches to trade is the different presumptions or rules regarding the role of governments. Free trade ideology encourages governments to have a neutral or hands-off rule (Laissez-faire of course, is the famous economic phrase) in choosing what a country imports and exports. The complex and elegant mechanisms of the free-market theory mean that the rule is that it is prices which act as the decision-making factor, as a complex system of self-interested choices automatically motivates a country to export what it is relatively most efficient at producing. Relative prices can reflect a country's natural and man-made assets, its skills, its relative prices of labour and other inputs, and therefore the market will search out and find what it 'should be' exporting and importing, without government direction. Therefore, under the free market, laissez-faire ideal, the rules are that the government's role is only to create the right conducive business conditions, like reasonable taxes, supportive business laws, and enforcement of contracts and property rights.

In a previous section, it was argued that the trade rules and policies of countries exist within a fragile, game theory-type of policy environment. In this environment, cooperating can be the best overall outcome, but countries also have a strong incentive to depart from the ideal rules when the risks or rewards are too great, or, in other words, cheat from a game theory point of view. The further factor highlighted in this section is that the situation of developing countries would obviously dispose them to wanting to be improving the level of expertise within their economies by using industrial and protectionist policies. Developing countries would wish to change the status quo of who presently is good at producing what, and would not be willing to follow passively forever the existing division of labour implied by submitting to free trade. And then if the developing country, like China today, is perceived by the already developed countries as being too aggressive or too successful at moving into desirable economic sectors like cars, then this disruption can trigger retaliation or protection of domestic developed country producers.

So all in all, I hope I have shown that the situation of the policies and attitudes of countries towards trade is a perennially unstable domain, with any discernible 'rules' based only on fragile foundations and, as history shows, easily abandoned in favour of domestic expediency. Into this unstable and fragile truce enters a growing China, with many millions of workers toiling away in thousands of factories with ever greater technological capabilities, and a government with unprecedented central control enacting the mother of all assertive industrial policy strategies.

CHAPTER TWO
China puts the Existing Rules-Based Trading System Under Pressure.

Many other countries before China used industrial policies, but China is a much larger country, and is not converging either in political values or its economic norms and structures.

During the post-war decades, there have been continuous examples of countries straying from free market rules to enact targeted industrial policies and successfully growing companies capable of exporting into Western markets. Japan and then the four so-called 'Asian Tigers', including most notably South Korea, are the most extreme and successful examples of following this industrial policy and export-led growth playbook. Like China in present times, Japan four decades ago was a country whose competitive manufacturing exports were causing waves of concern in developed countries, and Japan also grew at an average of 10% in the 15 years after WTO accession.[1] Japan was also accepted into the WTO with caution and voices of concern, with the US supporting the move partly for Cold War motives.[2] At that time, Japan also generated complaints from its trading partners about the difficulty of foreign firms being able to penetrate its domestic markets, and the technology transfer and industrial policy objectives shaping their economic relations. It was common at the time for some in American business to label Japan as 'Japan Inc.', signifying the prominence of Japan's industrial policy goals, and Japan's famously powerful industrial planning organisation, MITI, which had wide tentacles of influence into key areas of business and in dictating what could be imported or exported.

In 1985, the Plaza Accord was a deal struck between the US and other major economies, including West Germany, Japan, Britain, and France, to reduce the exchange rate value of the dollar. The revaluation would make US exports to other countries cheaper, and imports into the US more expensive, thus helping to reduce the trade imbalance in both ways. The threat of the US applying harsh unilateral tariffs helped to bring Japan to the negotiation table. At the same time, the US government negotiated agreements putting quotas on Japan's car exports into the US.[3] These quotas encouraged Japanese companies to build car plants within the US, which have since made a valuable contribution to the US economy. One point to learn from the example of Japan is that the GATT/WTO has always had limited power and influence to force or lock in free market or free trade policies, but can only encourage them. Japan moved towards a Western-style of government and economy for other reasons and not due to WTO pressure. Over the decades, Japan reduced its state direction in the economy, and it had already started with a better Western-style political system and individual human rights than compared to China today, and moved further in this direction. In general, Japan and South Korea moved towards a Western system both economically and politically. Although Japan and South Korea were and are economic rivals to the US and Europe, in other ways, they are now and have been for decades, friendly allies.

With these previous examples, the comparative economic size at the time of America and Western Europe was able to more easily absorb the mercantilist rule-breaking, tolerating the aggressive exporting combined with protected home markets, which those countries maintained during key periods. But China, with its massive population, is now partaking in its version of mercantilist, targeted industrial policies, combined with export-led growth. While Japan, South Korea and the others gradually moved to differing degrees to Western-style free-market economies and liberal democracies, China has retrenched backwards to a more authoritarian government, and stronger government control over its companies. The situation with China is also more contentious when it can be argued that the US is indirectly funding, through its trade deficits, not just its economic rival, but possibly a future military adversary.[4] China's behaviour in business espionage, cyber crimes, and even its provocative military actions near contested territories provides a real risk of future military tension. Japan might have been the example many hoped China would match, but especially since President Xi became leader, China has not responded to the benefits of international economic integration in this way. Japan and South Korea have grown to have high wages and a high GDP per person, with therefore less scope to undercut trade in goods based on cheaper labour costs. In contrast, China is still firmly in the middle-income country bracket on per-person metrics, even though it is exporting a lot of high-end manufactured goods, which previously have implied a high wage economy. So compared to Japan and South Korea, China has a far larger population, is more centralised and statist, and is not a geopolitical ally reliant on US military protection.

The pattern of the US and Western Europe running trade deficits and helping developing countries develop economically through export-led growth has helped a lot of countries. But at the end of the day, if any country is consuming more than it is producing by running a trade deficit every year, the iron mathematical rules or economic identities of trade relationships mean that that country is paying for that extra consumption by exchanging its wealth in return, and it is therefore getting slightly poorer with each yearly trade deficit. If trading partners are not getting back goods or services in return for their exports, that must mean they are holding onto the importing country's currency and will use it to buy assets like government debt, and to a growing extent, companies and other assets. The US has been effectively cashing in a small portion of its wealth to exchange for its trade deficits most years for 30 years. That is more concerning if strong ideological differences exist with a country that is slowly buying up and accumulating tiny fractions of the assets of your country every year.[5] As the former Trump administration Trade Representative Robert Lighthizer says in his book, 'No Trade is Free': *"In some ways, we are rebuilding Asia, and we can't afford that anymore." p279*

China eventually joined the WTO in 2001, but its efforts and negotiations to join started much earlier, with much hesitation about the decision coming from existing WTO members. The negotiation process required China to dramatically modify and reform the workings of aspects of its economy and trading practices, to make a move towards a more open and free market system. Joining the WTO required the negotiations to create a 'Protocol of Accession', which contained an official list of demands and requirements for China to meet, and China's protocol was understandably much more comprehensive than those demanded of other countries.[6] China's government did make many changes to its economy during this process, but arguably it did not change enough. Reconsidering these negotiations and the Protocol of Accession more than two decades later with the benefit of hindsight, it can be argued that many of today's trade conflicts with China can trace their source back to cracks and omissions in these negotiations.

A key factor noted by many who have studied the accession process is that many of the actors involved, and the wider political sentiments at the time, believed that China was on an irreversible path to a more Western-style free market economy, and the accession to the WTO would help that process along. There was a belief that even though there may be some gaps, ambiguities, and examples of unchallenged, outright central planning present in China at that time, the process of the population becoming richer, and of business and trade links becoming more influential within the country, meant that China would gradually but inevitably liberalise, both economically and politically. The thinking was that the business and consumerist Western-style capitalist values would gain in influence against the old Communist Party ideology. In other words, although the process was a fudge to some extent, the bet was that the overall long-term outcomes and trends would validate the WTO's goals in the end. The issues of China's government involvement in the economy were hiding in plain sight, but the Western leaders believed what they wanted to about the direction China would take. Some of that generation of Chinese reformers involved in the negotiations, who reportedly were offering calming reassurances during the discussions, might also themselves have believed that China was on a path of becoming more Westernised.[7]

"At the time that China entered the WTO, therefore, there was a clear awareness that China needed to continue to further its reforms. But, crucially, the vast majority of observers believed that accession to the WTO would, in itself, accelerate these reforms." 'China and the WTO' Movroidis & Sapir p25

"The WTO incumbents had likely taken it for granted that there was no going back from reforms. Recent experience put the lie to this assumption; nothing should be taken for granted when it comes to Chinese politics." 'China and the WTO' Movroidis & Sapir p203

(Note. The book 'China and the WTO' by Movroidis & Sapir has been drawn on heavily in this section of the essay, as it's a great guide to that complex subject, which I highly recommend. I think it's notable that one of the authors, Petros C. Movroidis, is a professor of 'Foreign and Comparative Law' and not economics, as the nuance of China's relationship with the WTO and the issues of rules being subtly broken or unable to be enforced, is perhaps better suited to a legal mind. In 2021, Prof Movroidis also did a great interview which is on YouTube based on the book, just type in 'China and the WTO'.)

If one frames the situation in terms of rules, then it is easy to see the WTO as a source of rules representing a particular free trade ideology, and China signing up to enjoy the benefits of being in that club but free-riding and never being willing to follow itself the obligations that the ideological rules imply. Again, the game theory interpretation is apt. The WTO's rules intend that countries be constrained from certain selfish trading behaviour in order for all to achieve a result which is second-best from an individual country perspective, but which maximises outcomes for the world economy as a whole. But China continued directing and subsidising its state-owned enterprises and private companies to defy the logic of free market prices, and instead plot a course towards its own industrial policy objectives.

"In China, rules are things to be managed and mitigated ... The dynamic is best summed up by the idiom 'Shang you zhengce, xia you duice: "From above there is policy, but from below there are countermeasures." Or, put another way, people can always find a way to get around the rules."
'China's Wall of Debt' Dinny McMahon p23-24

As the authors of 'China and the WTO' have emphasised, the creation of the GATT, which turned into the WTO, was predicated on a 'liberal understanding' of what and how a country's economy should operate and be managed. Right from the start, the main countries that designed and influenced the rules and intentions of the GATT were the US and UK, which both had an assumed, long-standing norm of having free market economies and a transparent and fair treatment of imports, with few impediments beyond straightforward and visible tariffs. In the US and UK, the implicit rules were that business was incentivised by market prices, and government interventions such as subsidies were restricted to specific economic sectors and clearly delineated actions when they became involved with commercial activities.[8] Part of the liberal understanding, therefore, is that there is an implicit assumption that when the companies within countries export goods, those goods will come from companies that are acting purely in response to commercial pressures and market prices and are not being subsidised or directed by government interests. As the authors of 'China and the WTO' put it: *"The quintessential element of the GATT is protecting the equality of competitive conditions."* p164 A key part of the liberal understanding therefore implies clear delineation lines between private commerce, which is privately owned businesses run on a profit maximisation basis within the laws and regulations of the land, and on the other hand government action, which has objectives other than profit, and in liberal understanding economies, is mostly confined to sectors with specific domestic 'free rider' or 'public good' dimensions, and not involved in the general exporting of manufactured goods. Of course, developed countries have broken their ideals and have and do often subsidise their exporters in certain instances, but the magnitude of these subsidies is small compared to China.

"What the liberal understanding amounts to is an acknowledgement that governments do not pre-empt the market mechanism." 'China and the WTO' Movroidis & Sapir p165

Start from this mindset, and it is clear that the way China's economy is designed and functions is the antithesis of this liberal understanding. All Chinese companies have explicit and implicit obligations and ties to the government/CCP. In 2017, the Chinese government made it law that all Chinese companies must follow the instructions of the government when asked to do so for special national interest reasons. The government/CCP leverages subsidies, law-making and other influences in the service of complex and all-important broader industrial policy goals to get companies to act in a way it wants. This is in contrast to the liberal understanding, where companies respond only to profitable opportunities. China's economy has many other facets that increase the influence of the government/CCP over companies. There are state holding companies that own and control businesses in key industries, state dominance in the banking sector, a national planning agency with broad powers, nimble linkages across firms coordinated by the State-owned Asset Supervision and Administration Commission (SASAC), state control over appointments in key companies, and the embedding of Party personnel on boards of private companies. Many countries in the past and present have done some of these, but only China has done all of them, the result being a government/CCP with unprecedented powers to steer a highly developed and very large economy.[9]

In the past there have been examples of countries that had economic systems at odds with WTO norms, and they were still allowed to join. But those countries were very small exporters, and in most cases, they moved towards Western economic norms over time. Even planned-economy Poland was allowed to join the GATT in 1967, with the non-free and open market issue being fudged over by means of an agreement to reciprocate exports with imports (if only China were importing as much as it exported to Western countries!). The Western powers were willing to fudge the implicit liberal understanding ethos the GATT was founded on, in return for a chance to disrupt the Soviet sphere of influence and promote free market values. Also, Poland's small economy and limited exporting capabilities at that time were not a large threat.[10] Like many international organisations, geopolitical expediencies and expectations of future trends convinced the incumbent countries of the GATT/WTO that encouraging China along the better path was worth compromising its rules. One viewpoint was that China could join the WTO under a fudge of compromise, and then, once within the international capitalist free market system, the benefits and interests of commerce would pull China towards liberal understanding policies and free market economic structures. But this fudge at first, and then tempt and improve modus has not worked with China, leaving some, including the authors of 'China and the WTO' believing that the liberal understanding assumptions in the foundations of WTO thinking need to be more definitively noted, emphasised, and expressed in legal and contractual language, if the WTO is ever going to maintain a multilateral, free market trading system.

"The WTO Agreement, like the original GATT Agreement (1947), is silent about state ownership and, more broadly, about state involvement in the trading regime. This reflected the fact that the GATT's main architects were Americans and British, the foremost market economies, and that all its original participants shared (or at least accepted) a liberal understanding of law and democracy." 'China and the WTO' Movroidis & Sapir p68

"The liberal understanding does permeate the GATT/WTO regime. It is the spirit of the GATT that China is violating through its policies with respect to SOEs and forced Technology Transfer. Under the circumstances, the trading community could not stay idle. Sooner or later, the crisis had to knock on the door of the WTO house. ... The world community is in search of a solution." 'China and the WTO' Movroidis & Sapir p172

"there is a need to translate some of the liberal understanding of the law, which was implicit in the GATT era and remains implicit today in the WTO, into operational rules so as to ensure that China and WTO members that belong to a different tradition of the law fit better with the WTO than they actually do." 'China and the WTO' Movroidis & Sapir p192

Subsidies are a big issue for China's trading partners, leading to the related dispute over whether China's State Owned Enterprises can be considered 'Public Bodies' that give out subsidies.

Government subsidies are something that the rules and ethos of the WTO pay close attention to. Obviously, if free trade means markets acting only on the basis of free market prices, which are derived from legitimate market costs and benefits on a level playing field, then government subsidies are suspect number one in distorting company behaviour, and hence distorting the patterns of trade. After all, this is usually the motive behind the subsidies in the first place. Within the key WTO rules and decision-making structures, the identification of a government awarding a subsidy is only confirmed if it can be asserted that the organisation awarding or passing on the subsidy is a 'public body'. To what extent China's SOEs can be claimed to be public bodies has therefore been the centre of a great deal of dispute in recent years, and the WTO has been accused of being inconsistent. This area is a main source of the dissatisfaction the US and others have had with the WTO. At one point, the US was pushing to claim that most Chinese SOEs were de facto public bodies for the purposes of the rules. Meanwhile, the WTO took the opposite view, leaving the Chinese free to channel subsidies through their SOEs. It was this difference of interpretation and opinion that soured the relationship between the US and the WTO Appellate Body, which is the final arbiter of judgments in this area.[11]

"The United States has, wrongly, decided to simply equate state ownership with unmarket-like behaviour without determining whether a particular state-owned company behaved like a private company or not. The WTO Appellate Body was, originally at least, equally wrong to ignore state ownership. Consequently, the Appellate Body would not see anything wrong with state ownership and would routinely find against the United States every time it equated state-owned companies with subsidizing agents." 'China and the WTO' Movroidis & Sapir p183

"The court concluded that subsidies from state-owned enterprises were not automatically subsidies from the state, and so not covered by the WTO's ban. In effect, the Chinese state was free to subsidize exporters and import-competing firms, provided it worked through businesses or other organs that could be held, as a matter of law, to be at arm's length." 'Global Discord' Paul Tucker p402

In a Western-style economy, where most commerce is carried out by privately owned companies, and government involvement is clearly delineated and identified, this 'public body' distinction is pretty straightforward. In looking for evidence of subsidy in a Western-type economy, the WTO would check if any alleged benefit was linked to any national or regional government body or any quango, and then could safely assume that any commercial company outside this group would not have any motives to be providing a subsidy. In the Western economy way of thinking, there are two clear groupings: private businesses act on the incentives of prices and profits, while governments act on the basis of their wider and more long-term goals, which can include industrial policies. But subsidies in a complex economic system like China's are not always clearly labelled or delineated as a direct payment from government to a business and can include more subtle benefits, such as cheap land or rent, tax breaks, cheap energy, or cheap material inputs. Trying to ascertain what is a subsidy and what is not requires one to interpret the ideology and theory of what are free markets and real or true prices, and apply these theories to the messy practical business world. So, for example, a country having a low tax system is legitimate, but a country giving tax breaks to specific exporting companies is not.

The characteristics of a public body within this context includes an organisation lacking the profit motive as the main driver of its behaviour, and having a 'soft budget constraint', where an organisation is not reliant on private capitalists, who are naturally hoping to be paid back returns for their capital outlay.[12] In China, most credit is de facto controlled by provincial and municipal governments, which certainly equates to easy terms and soft budget constraints for a sister company SOE in the same region.[13] In Western capitalist economies, this delineation between the private/commercial and government spheres is fairly clear. In China, however, and especially recently with Communist Party influence being expanded further into nominally private sector companies, the delineation is far from clear. The notions initially supported by 1980s Chinese leader Deng Xiaoping of separating the Communist Party from the bureaucratic side of government and separating government from business have been abandoned, with ever more pervasive Party intrusion into SOEs and private sector businesses in the last decade.[14] So for these reasons, in China, it is inevitably far more difficult to ascertain whether the rules and ideals of free trade and free markets have been broken due to 'public bodies' subsidising private commercial businesses, who are then exporting or competing with other countries' imports within China. Economists who have studied these questions have calculated that China's subsidies are very large. *"According to a very conservative estimate, industrial subsidies in China amounted to around EUR221billion or 1.73% of Chinese GDP in 2019."* 'Foul Play? On the Scale and Scope of Industrial Subsidies in China' by Bickenbach, Dohse, Langhammer, and Liu. Kiel Institute publication online.

"Are SOEs private agents or public bodies? ... Like a stone in the shoe, this unanswered question is an irritant right at the point of closest contact between WTO members." 'China and the WTO' Movroidis & Sapir p82

"If the Party is lord of all it surveys, does that mean that everything that goes on in the PRC is governmental, or attributable to state policy or actions? There is simply no sensible answer to this that fits into the usual principles of market exchange." 'Global Discord' Paul Tucker p403

"the Agreement on Subsidies and Countervailing Measures is the legal instrument in the WTO context that most drastically calls for a halt to government intervention. And yet, surprisingly, this agreement does not explicitly mention SOEs. The SCM aims to discipline financial contributions by public bodies to the extent that they confer benefits to specific recipients. Arguably, SOEs could be considered

"public bodies", the subject matter of the SCM, but as previously discussed, the understanding of this term has caused considerable acrimony." 'China and the WTO' Movroidis & Sapir p60

"China's State Owned Enterprises are the epitome of deeply vested interests, with no small degree of cosy corruption deeply embedded within them. The symbiotic relationship between SOEs and state banks is a form of protectionism that will be very difficult to break." 'China's Future' David Shambaugh p42

Another contention is the way China has used 'Forced Technology Transfer', to gain manufacturing knowledge and capability from developed country companies wishing to sell into China.

Apart from the issue of China's SOEs being a covert source of unfair subsidy, the other big issue upsetting China's trade partners is the way China has forced developed country companies to transfer their technological knowledge and capabilities to Chinese companies. The pattern is for China to offer access to its domestic market to developed country companies, strictly conditional on partnering with Chinese companies, and/or using Chinese companies as suppliers. The Chinese companies are then encouraged to become competent in this technology, and gradually over time, the companies within the sector are encouraged to produce a competing product, using less or not using at all the initial developed-country company in the supply chain. In this process, it has often been claimed that agreements and/or intellectual property laws have been compromised or flouted. The hoped-for Chinese markets for the developed-country company might be good at first, but after a while, domestic alternatives become more popular. Exporters to China suffer from the opaque industrial policy 'Made in China' interests at every turn, and which sentiments are pervasive across the Chinese business environment. In an asymmetry worrying for developed economies, developed country companies arguably consider only their own commercial interests and medium-term profits, and not their home country's long-term interests, when deciding to do business in China (see later section on Apple). In contrast, Chinese companies are forced by the pervasive influence of the CCP to focus on long-term Chinese nationalist industrial policy goals. There have been many instances of technology developed in developed economies, sometimes even with government support, ending up with Chinese companies dominating the markets. Arguably, some developed-country companies have been too silent about the bad-faith actions happening in China, for fear of the consequences harming their business position and relations.[15]

"these two issues [SOEs and technology transfer] capture almost to perfection the hybrid nature of "public-private partnership" that permeates the Chinese economy and has given rise to the vast majority of complaints raised against China since its accession." 'China and the WTO' Movroidis & Sapir p61

"over time and for foreign firms especially, 'indigenous innovation' came to be associated with various forms of protectionism and favouritism for local companies, unfair trade and commercial practices, and... 'a blueprint for technology theft on a scale the world has never seen before.'" 'Red Flags' George Magnus 146-7

"Then chief executive officer Josef Kaeser of Siemens, a German industrial company, explained in an interview: "The Chinese go into a company, give job guarantees, and everyone's reassured. At some point, another company is founded in which the old one is absorbed, and research and development are stripped away."" 'Trade Wars' Oermann & Wolff p167

"Once China entered the WTO in 2001, however, explicitly conditioning market access on tech transfer was illegal in most sectors. As President Clinton had put it: "We don't have to transfer technology or do joint manufacturing in China anymore." But the practice didn't really end; instead, the pressure turned informal. The Chinese market was so large that foreign companies would sometimes "voluntarily" enter such agreements. A textbook example occurred in the early 2000s when China planned the largest high-speed rail network in the world. The potential orders to foreign companies were enormous, creating a Prisoner's Dilemma among Siemens, Bombardier, and Kawasaki. In the end, all three agreed to transfer technology to state-backed companies in exchange for market access. By 2010, policy had shifted to favour local industry; the foreign companies struggled to compete in China, and the local companies began exporting their technology abroad. As one Japanese executive involved put it "[The Japanese and Europeans] were afraid this situation would happen in the future, but they thought it would take more time. The Chinese catch-up speed was so fast; they could not have imagined they would be competing [with the Chinese] for contracts in the US." 'Apple in China' Patrick McGee p240

China's opaque structures and the lack of delineation between its ever more pervasive government and commercial activity make proving breaches of the rules difficult.

The Protocol of Accession, which China had to negotiate before being allowed to join the WTO, included clauses aiming to guard against forced technology transfer (FTT). But the rules were and are focused only on protecting against 'public bodies' partaking in forced technology transfer. The rules and clauses are not adequately tailored to the many grey areas and pervasive industrial policy pressures China's companies act under. Just like the contention over whether SOEs can be considered public bodies, the issues surrounding China using FTT are complicated by trying to apply rules and norms that assume a clear delineation between private/commercial and government/public bodies to a country with a system where these lines are blurred or non-existent. To bring a case against China, another country has to prove that the Chinese government has used unfair, forceful methods to transfer technology from the foreign company to Chinese companies. But if there is no way of implicating the Chinese government's fingerprints directly in the chain of events, then the WTO and its rules and sanctions are toothless. If the FTT seemed to be enacted at the company level by the supposedly 'private' Chinese companies partnering with the developed country companies, then the WTO and its rules are not triggered.[16] The behaviour of private companies falls under internal domestic competition law, which is not covered by the WTO, as the WTO's focus is more on the behaviour of governments and the relationships between countries.[17]

There is a common thread running through these issues, where it seems that China's uniquely opaque and complex economic and political environment makes applying economic rules designed for other countries difficult. Besides the SOEs and forced technology transfer issues discussed above, the issue over the difficulty of importing into China is another example. Although on paper basic tariffs might not be that high, and other countries' imports might seem, in theory, to be free to be sold within China, opaque and informal systems and connections in reality make it hard and favour domestic companies at every turn. For a start, goods from foreign companies can only be sold through a Chinese partner and/or a state distributor, thus providing an initial avenue or choke point for friction and drag to be placed upon foreign imports. Again, there is subjective behaviour and de facto realities which are against the spirit of the WTO free trade and free market ethos, but which escape any of the WTO's objective rules and sanctions due to the opacity and nuance of the Chinese economic system. It is not easy to prove foul play was at work when, at different stages of the retail chain, domestic alternatives were chosen over your imports, as free choice is an accepted part of any market system. But whatever the Chinese government claims otherwise, at the end of the day, the proof is in the trade numbers.

"With the allure of its giant market, Beijing has been able to insist on bespoke terms in its own investment treaties (e.g., requiring most inward investment via joint ventures), to shrug off limited WTO obligations, and to escape legal challenges given the burdens of assembling concrete, usable evidence (and the risk of complainants triggering cases against their home states). 'Global Discord' Paul Tucker p420

Within the GATT/WTO body of rules and laws, there are many tools for a country to use to protect itself from disruptive surges of imports. But when it comes to using rules and laws to ensure other countries' markets are open for reciprocal exports, the system is weak, and the standard for demonstrating instances of discrimination is hard to meet. The WTO on its own has no investigative enforcement powers within countries' borders, and relies on complainant countries collecting evidence.[18] Long-winded WTO investigations of possible rule-breaking can take so long to establish that by the time a prosecution is concluded, harmed businesses might already be financially bust, and benefiting businesses might have already established a competitive and first-mover advantage in their markets.[19] In this case, justice delayed is indeed justice denied. The policing of certain unfair practices may rely on local Chinese courts to protect the rights of foreign companies in China. But given the pervasiveness of the CCP and its industrial policy goals, expecting independent judgments is unrealistic. The Party is everywhere. China's record regarding how relatively few (compared to the size of its trade) cases it has had brought against it and how willing it has been to seem to respond positively to those judgments, taken at face value, does not reflect the controversy it is generating among its trading partners. This lack of cases brought against China is more a reflection of the limited scope of WTO rules and the opaqueness of China's system, than it is a positive reflection on China's compliance with the 'spirit' of WTO rules.[20]

"There is recent evidence, indeed, that despite having on paper a competition regime similar to that of the EU, China nonetheless manages to treat Chinese companies differently from foreign companies operating in its market through other instruments." 'China and the WTO' Movroidis & Sapir p215

One way to view the situation from a theoretical perspective is to assert that because China does not follow the foundational rules of a Western-style free market economy, this ironically makes accusations of breaking secondary WTO-type, free trade rules harder to prove. It is harder to prove unfair government support of private commerce if there is less clear delineation between government and private commerce in the first place, as one would expect in a market economy, and as those countries that created the WTO rules assumed. Cases are hard to bring against China's system because the factors involved are so opaque, with the workings of business, economic decision-making, and even more practical aspects like prices for all the inputs involved in business, hard to define. In China, all economic factors and actors exist in a soup of bureaucratic objectives and government relationships and distortions, meaning many areas of business are not reliant on free market prices. These include, most significantly, China's ambitious industrial policies, which are the antithesis to the free market, level playing field ethos of the WTO.

An analogy could be made with the subject of tax accountancy. The person who gets charged with tax fraud is done so by the evidence of a recorded trail of transactions, which their society and the norms of their business environment require them to make. But if that person was able to make money in a way in which no such trail of transactions was available to the tax authorities, such as trading in a black-market way using only cash and no paper records, then the tax authorities would not deem it worth their while trying to make a case against them. They would decide that they could not produce the paper trail of evidence needed for a prosecution. Investigations into offshore tax evasion schemes are notable for the creation of complexity and subterfuge, which the perpetrators create in order to make it more difficult for the authorities to prove wrongdoing. The irony, therefore in China's case, is that in not following the basic rules by which Western-style free market economies operate, scrutinising China in terms of more subtle free market WTO-type rules is subsequently harder. Without the separation of powers in the political system, without only specific linkages between business and government, without trustworthy company accounts, and without transparent free market prices, proving wrongdoing is difficult. Without these basic attributes of free market economies in place, it is impossible to scrutinise as to whether China is complying with further, more subtle, second-tier rules, such as the free trade rules created by the WTO club.

"in China the visible hand doesn't simply build a framework. In the interests of achieving the outcomes it wants, it meddles constantly. The presence of the visible hand is so pervasive that the Chinese instead refer to it as 'xian bu zhu de shou': 'the restless hand'." 'China's Wall of Debt' Dinny McMahon p12

The first Trump administration departed from the norms of the WTO, and instead acted and negotiated on trade issues unilaterally and more assertively.

China's exports were and are cheap for three main reasons. First, through them having low wages, which, although rising steadily, still statistically represents a smaller than usual share for labour from their country's economic rewards. Secondly, to a different extent over the years, and especially from roughly 2004–2014, China had a currency exchange rate that was lower than it should have been. This is due to deliberate policy interventions which redirected or sucked up the dollars earned by exporting companies, preventing the natural evolution of the exchange rate to a higher level, which strong exports should cause. Thirdly, industrial policy subsidies from China's government subsidise exporters, meaning they do not need to see such high returns for their exports, and can instead focus on gaining market share and economies of scale.

As China's exports into the US grew, there were some mainstream economists who took the view that if China wanted to sell its goods to the US at prices which were theoretically too cheap, then this was a benefit to US consumers, and while it may be disruptive to manufacturers, it would be a matter of adjusting and would not be necessarily damaging to the US economy in the long run. Those against protectionist policies assert that often more jobs are lost to technological change than trade, which is a valid point. Purist free traders also believe market forces will always find new sectors and new jobs for those displaced by imports. To some extent, this has been proven true throughout history, as trade and technology have gradually and consistently changed the jobs available to the population (i.e., there used to be a lot of farmers). But the quite dramatic loss of American manufacturing jobs, from what was later labelled 'the China shock', changed the sentiments for many within the US, as more jobs were lost and fewer new ones took their place compared to what economists had predicted. The loss of jobs was concentrated in certain Midwest regions reliant on manufacturing employment, while the new growth sectors provided few well-paid jobs, spread around already prosperous regions, and many low-paid jobs in services.

The first Trump administration enacted a radical change of course in terms of its approach to trading with China. A key narrative of the Trump campaign had been 'America First', and Trump had famously quipped that the US must stop being a 'sucker' for passively letting China run up the US trade deficit, partly by its deliberate industrial policies. In previous years, the US had already been seriously dissatisfied with aspects of China's behaviour in the areas of subsidies, and the treatment of companies doing business in or with China who experienced forced technology transfer, and impediments to accessing Chinese consumers. Also, the US had already previously complained about the lack of pushback towards China's practices from the WTO and the decisions when they were made, seeming not to be in accordance with the spirit of Western free trade values and norms (aka the liberal understanding).

The US, with its large, lucrative consumer market, has been a major target of WTO litigation by other countries wishing to export more, and therefore was the most frequently sued country at the WTO.[21] This seems unfair when, before the Trump tariffs, the US had notably lower tariffs than its trading partners, and even supposedly economically liberal partners like the EU. It could also be deemed unfair when the US trade deficit inherently implied the US was not being a bad-faith player of the trade game. Meanwhile, China attracted fewer than its share of dispute claims, arguably because, as discussed above, the nature of its opaque economic structures and internal business relationships made pinning down wrongdoing difficult. China and others had chosen to take the path where litigating using WTO rules was a more beneficial route to trade gains than the older modes of negotiating trade deals.[22] It is commendable that the WTO includes concessions for developing countries, allowing them more leeway in their trade policies. But it is questionable that a country like China should be allowed under WTO rules to 'self-designate' as a developing country.[23] A word that cuts into the real issues surrounding China and trade is reciprocity. China's determined and potent industrial policy goals and stances, mean there are many areas where they benefit from access to foreign markets, but where China limits access to its own market. US tech markets are one visible example, where Amazon and Google are banned in China, while WeChat, TikTok, and Alibaba are allowed to operate in the US.[24]

The Trump administration took the controversial step of refusing to endorse judges for the WTO's Appellate Body, a key decision-making body within the WTO that adjudicates on trade disputes. This meant that after the existing judges' terms had expired, the US veto on all new judges meant the Appellate Body was no longer available to make judgments about trade disputes. It was this Appellate Body which had, in the eyes of the US, failed to make the correct judgments about China's SOEs being 'Public Bodies', in the disputes regarding whether they were therefore a legitimate focus for claims of unfair subsidies under WTO rules. To critics, the Appellate Body had not merely sought to interpret WTO rules but saw itself as perfecting and expanding the rules, which critics believed was beyond their remit.[25] Without the Appellate Body, the WTO has lost a key part of its enforcement structure, but it still has other institutional powers with which it has limped on in its role of trying to police international trade. The 'panel process', which has always tried to settle disputes before they get to the Appellate Body, is still being presented with cases to look into and is still making pronouncements on these cases, based partly on the precedents and jurisprudence which the Appellate Body has concluded in previous cases.

The first Trump administration used Section 301 tariffs against China, the US legislation for which had been created in 1974 and intended to be used to respond to unfair trade practices and protect domestic interests. Section 301 tariffs were used extensively in the 1980s and early 1990s, but before President Trump, no Section 301 tariffs had been used since the creation of the WTO in 1994. During these earlier tariff actions, different US administrations felt that countries, most notably then Japan, were generating a damaging level of imports and harming US industry. For example, President G.H.W. Bush had used Section 301 tariffs against Japan in 1989.[26] Compared to the 'toothless' GATT, the new enforcement powers of the WTO after 1994 gave a new route to solving trade disputes, as it now had the capability to impose sanctions. This sanction capability of the new WTO supposedly replaced the need to resort to actions like the US Section 301 tariffs, until the Trump administration lost faith in the WTO route and decided to return to using unilateral action.

Supporters of the moves of the first Trump administration would argue that this can be thought of as a point when the US was no longer willing to be the passive player or victim in the trade game. From their point of view, the US had been continuing to act in line with the ideal collaborative solution for everyone, but was being taken advantage of by other players cheating in the game. This thinking would justify Trump's 'sucker' comments. One factor of the rules-based WTO system, and one which makes it attractive to smaller countries, is that having common rules reduces the power of large countries to use their size to get better conditions for themselves. But with the US already having comparatively low import tariffs compared to other countries, and a transparent and consumer-oriented market economy, further free trade agreements held little attraction for other countries, as the US was already letting in foreign goods easily. It could be argued that the Chinese and other countries that were and are contributing to the US trade deficit were failing to make any concessions or interested in making any new free trade deals because the US already had low tariffs in most areas.

The Trump administration changed the landscape of its trade relationships by being willing to take away, or threaten to take away, the easy access to its consumer and business markets from foreign exporters. It was therefore recasting US market access as a prize to be earned, rather than a given to be assumed.[27] In being willing to impose unilateral tariffs and neutering the WTO's Appellate Body, the Trump administration was signalling that it was exiting the WTO mindset and reasserting the implicit card it can play against other countries, who want a part of its consumer markets. Although tariffs and their tendency to lead to retaliation insinuate negative connotations for most economists and students of history, the experience of the Trump administration robustly negotiating trade issues with China and others did produce positive concessions. There were some examples where trade partners were previously obfuscating and delaying, and backtracking on fruitless talks, but who suddenly came quickly to the negotiating table when the US created instant leverage by threatening to curtail their easy access to US markets.[28] Although the realm of tariffs and protection is distasteful to most economists, the scale and trend of the US trade deficit and the realities of trade with China especially, help to justify the motives for these controversial steps. The legitimacy of the Trump tariffs is also supported by the fact that in the retaliation game which followed, China came close to running out of ammo in terms of retaliatory tariffs to impose because, revealingly, it just does not buy that much goods from the US, which illustrates the core of the matter.[29]

The trade war started by the first Trump administration helped to create the trend for partial decoupling and friend-shoring regarding China, as the pattern of the ever-closer economic interactions of both trade and investment of previous decades was halted. The US and other Western countries are going further in decoupling their economies and production structures from China in key sectors, especially where national security or special technology considerations are in play. But as ex-Australian Prime Minister and avid China student Kevin Rudd noted, this is only doing the same as what China and its industrial policy are already doing, in what he calls "decoupling with Chinese characteristics."[30] The combination of China's policies, pervasive government control, and its authoritarian values means it presents the biggest threat to the US and others since the Soviet Union, while the contrast is that there were fewer economic ties across those Cold War battle lines. This means the US and others should and are looking carefully at all aspects of economic ties, including incoming and outgoing investment relationships.[31]

The most controversial trade action the first Trump administration took was its tariffs on steel and aluminium, which were Section 232 tariffs. These are based on earlier US legislation from 1962 and have a 'national security' component, unlike the Section 301 tariffs. One reason these steel and aluminium tariffs were so contentious was that they affected trade with Canada and Mexico. This was because US decision makers judged that the markets for these two products are so seriously affected by China's surplus capacity and dumping abroad, that it would have a knock-on effect on Canada and Mexico's trading behaviour with the US.[32]

Critics of what the first Trump administration actually did regarding trade and tariffs argue that rather than pushing for systematic improvements in the way the WTO manages these areas, such as SOE subsidies or forced technology transfer, the US ended up reducing the global power and influence of the free market norms and ideals represented by the WTO.[33] Rather than using threats of access to America's valuable consumer market as a stick to push for improved rules and action in the direction of WTO and liberal understanding-type concepts, the Trump administration's actions seem more like old-fashioned, self-interested protectionism. For example, the Trump administration demanding China meet specific targets for increased imports from the US was old-fashioned national self-interest, and not dealing with systemic issues to improve the wider trading system or China's behaviour within it. On the whole, the tariffs and other re-shoring initiatives had very limited success, with, for example, one study concluding that a maximum of 12,700 steel jobs were preserved but at a technical economic cost to the wider economy of $900,000 per job when the increased steel prices are factored in.[34] But because the wider costs are spread into tiny amounts for the whole population, while the gains are concentrated in certain small groups and even certain political regions, the politician might see the action as politically rewarding. Further arguments which complicate the issues can be made, especially in a key sector like steel, in which there can be national reasons why a capacity to make one's own steel is worth paying a price for. This argument is reinforced if world prices are deemed to be subsidized as part of a competitor country's strategic industrial policy to gain market share, and therefore not guaranteed to be forever low.

In acting unilaterally and with such a simplistic 'America First' style, although kind of justified by the trade deficit and China's behaviour, the first Trump administration's actions risk losing the moral high ground. China's disruption of the common good free trade ideals is less conspicuous if America has also abandoned them. Understandably, Beijing fears 'issue-based coalitions' where the bulk of the developed world disagrees with China. But Trump's unilateral actions are a step away from any international coalition sentiments being nurtured.[35] These self-interested negotiations can be argued to be a step back towards 'might is right' trade relations, in contrast to a rules-based system represented in the goals of the WTO. As the authors of China and the WTO argue, the game would be more effectively played by the WTO representing the common good interests of many countries, and not the unilateral actions of the US.[36] The US acting alone undermined the most powerful weapon against China's policies, which would be a wider international rallying behind support for better trade practices. As the quote below illustrates, the Trump administration so blatantly sidelining the WTO has undermined its legitimacy, and smaller countries cannot be expected to abide by rules that they find uncomfortable if they see the US ignore previous commitments when it suits.

"President Trump's policies had the opposite effect. By violating fundamental rules and norms of the system himself, he invited others to follow suit (and emulate many of China's proclivities, including trade and investment restrictions) and jeopardized its basic institutional foundations." 'The United States vs China' C. Fred Bergsten p23

But Trump supporters, like his former trade representative Robert Lighthizer, whose book has been cited in this essay, argue that during those years, with America's potential allies on relatively good terms with China and not (yet) in the same mindset as the US, acting with allies through the WTO was not then practical. For example, at that time, Angela Merkel's German government was mindful of the boom in German exporting of high-end manufactured goods and machinery into China and had a strong EU influence. Multilateral actions and/or using the WTO route at that time, Lighthizer argues, would have taken much negotiation and delay and would have struggled to provide the instant leverage and power to negotiations that unilateral US Section 301 tariffs did.[37] Now the potential allies, like Germany, might be more sceptical in their sentiments towards China, as they see China's industrial policies copy then replace their high-end goods, and the trading relationship now looks less rosy.

"The Europeans and other middle powers have demonstrated an ability to protect systemic stability, even during the recent period of US leadership abdication, and surely can continue to do so with a partial US return." 'The United States vs China' C. Fred Bergsten p280

"Essentially, the Chinese are moving away from interdependence and toward a relationship where they supply us as they want and develop and produce on their own in important sectors." 'No Trade is Free' Robert Lighthizer p211

"At present, the WTO membership knows that any time a big player is unhappy with the state of affairs, irrespective of whether the source of unhappiness is legitimate or not, it can simply step out of the system until it has worked out a solution to its liking. The thrust of the game, thus could be interpreted as the search not for cooperative solutions that will benefit some today and others tomorrow but for solutions that will always make the same people happy. What is the incentive of third parties to invest in such an endeavour, unless their interests are aligned with those of the major trading powers? The whole idea of a rules-based system was to establish a framework that would apply to all, irrespective of size and bargaining power." 'China and the WTO' Movroidis & Sapir p150

The Biden administration maintained the stance of Trump's trade policies, but with more emphasis on subsidies rather than further tariff threats, and with more emphasis on gaining allies abroad.

The Biden administration was less aggressive in its threats of further tariffs with China, but it refused to draw down the existing tariffs and rewind conditions back to 2016, as some might have hoped. Therefore, it could be said that the more assertive approach to trade with China which Trump initiated, evolved rather than reversed, as the Biden administration went big into a modern industrial and innovation strategy, enacting huge subsidies and government investment. The assertiveness was still there, but it shifted emphasis from tariffs on imports to government support for key areas of domestic manufacturing.

The central policy was the Inflation Reduction Act, the name being arguably misleading, as it was broadly about subsidies and a proactive industrial policy and not reducing inflation. The aim of the policies within the act was to help protect existing manufacturing capacity and build new capacity in key green and high-tech sectors, maintaining competitiveness with China, and trying to maintain and create good manufacturing jobs. As Jake Sullivan, President Biden's National Security Advisor, noted Biden saying, when he hears the word "climate," he thinks "jobs". Sullivan also labelled the administration's policies as "foreign policy for the middle class", highlighting the emphasis on the hope for more well-paid manufacturing jobs.[38] Rather than the old free market criticism that government investment 'crowds out' private investment, the Biden administration was expressing an intention to 'crowd in' private investment, as the government investment helps to build clusters of capabilities and capacities that have high growth and export potential.

Most economists support some kind of carbon tax as the solution to achieve green goals efficiently. But it is politically unattractive as a policy because it creates a big new painful tax for consumers and businesses. Arguably, the thrust of the subsidies in the IRA offered a more politically attractive route towards the green objectives, which subsidise green options, rather than penalising non-green fossil fuel options. The subsidies hoped to create new businesses and jobs, and these would act as political interest groupings that would embed the support for green industry. The outcome of the international subsidy war as different countries vie to become major players in these new, promising sectors is actually still good for green objectives, even if free trade ideals are being trampled. Another point is that the 2022 CHIPS and Science Act in the US, which seeks to subsidise and keep healthy the US microchip sector, was also part of the broader industrial policy moves.

Those moves and the big subsidy thrust of the Inflation Reduction Act still, however, represent a departure from the implicit rules of free trade, and suggest the tide has changed in the US's long-term trade policy stance. The ethos of free trade, which the WTO is based on, would want governments to stay out of commercial decisions and the competitive trade arena, but the IRA brings government right back to centre. The Biden administration policies and narratives were aiming to be more sensitive and cooperative to allied countries compared to the first Trump administration, but the scale of subsidies enacted inevitably drew reactions from trading partners like the EU, who are sensitive to advantages given to American producers in key promising economic sectors, which they inevitably also want to be present and successful in. However, it's worth remembering that the resurgent industrial policy in the US has not changed the delineation between government support and private commerce, which is still very clear in the US, in contrast with opaque China.

"A modern American industrial strategy identifies sectors that are foundational to economic growth, strategic from a national security perspective, and where private industry on its own isn't poised to make the investments needed to secure our national ambitions." Jake Sullivan speech April 27th 2023

"These are tailored measures. They are not, as Beijing says, a "technology blockade." They are not targeting emerging economies. They are focused on a narrow slice of technology and a small number of countries intent on challenging us militarily." Jake Sullivan speech April 27th 2023

"We thought we were in the era of free market globalization, and now we are not" Martin Wolf FT YouTube IRA.

CHAPTER THREE
How to Think About the Rules for International Trade in a Post-Successful China World.

The traditional argument of the free-market economist is that governments have a poor record of 'picking winners', but for China, 'Green' sectors have been a good bet.

The traditional retort of the free-market supporter when arguing against using industrial policies and infant industry policies, is that governments have poor abilities and a poor track record in 'picking winners'. In other words, the ecology made up of networks of free-thinking, enterprising individuals and capitalist companies, under the incentive of profit and competition, are far better at finding, developing and commercialising new goods and services than bureaucratic government departments. Governments end up clumsily throwing government money at what they guess will be the next big thing, and getting it wrong. Also, planned economies are traditionally thought of as being capable of copying existing goods and services, but not good at developing innovative new areas where the best profits and spillovers can be found. These were some of the key conclusions reached regarding the worsening economic underperformance of the Soviet Union and communist Eastern European countries a few decades ago. Planned economies can be good at harnessing their resources towards big clear objectives, but not good at being innovative and responsive when it comes to the complex, evolving demands of a modern mass consumer society. A key point when remembering the Soviet Union, was that when they set themselves clear and relatively one-dimensional goals, like, for the most impressive examples, putting a man into space or building up their military, including nuclear weapons, they were actually able to perform quite well. But at the same time, to be a Soviet consumer was disappointing.

"It is not hard to see China's authoritarian economy succeeding in some of its new industrial endeavours, ... The Soviet Union, for example, was no slouch when it came to science, space, engineering and research and development. ... And yet, these were not enough." 'Red Flags' George Magnus p137

As a semi-planned economy trying to pick winners, one of the wisest and most consequential sets of moves China has made has been in the direction of green solar and wind energy, electric vehicles and batteries. After all, if one is searching for future trends in profitable business, then the growing concern for climate change and environmental pollution makes green investment and innovation a great bet in the winner-picking game. For example, it did not take much of a searching and responsive business ecology to predict that solar panels would grow in economic importance across the world. It was a sure bet made in China on a large scale from top down, and it worked. There was and is little subtle consumer taste to respond to; just throw everything at making the cheapest solar panels possible, which can produce the most electricity possible, and on a suitably competition-crushing scale. China's domination of the production of solar panels is a key example of how it used its industrial policy to become a big player and then had the capability to crush Western competition through low prices and economies of scale.

Knowing that Western car giants had an insurmountable advantage in combustion engine cars, years before it was such a big deal, China directed and made subsidies and cheap finance available to many companies investing in electric vehicle and battery development and production. What China lacks in the sensitive, opportunity-seeking strengths of a capitalist, entrepreneurial ecosystem, it makes up for in the sheer heft of potential government subsidy and finance, and joined-up national mobilisation of its economy towards targeted goals. A semi-planned economy like China can place all their chips on certain good bets and be confident that they can crush the competition out of the market. Even when many other developed countries are arriving at the same green winner-picking conclusions, China can conclude that it can out-subsidise, out-invest, out-scale and out-control the supply chain (for example for batteries partly by cornering key rare earth inputs). The way China's government dictates and directs its economy into these areas where it has ambitions is reminiscent of the US or UK mobilisations during WWII, when the economy was steered away from serving normal consumer wants, towards military and national objectives dictated by their governments. Government officials were given unprecedented authority to intervene, confiscate and mobilise in the commercial economy. China's economy is kind of on this economic war-like footing permanently.

A large part of the Biden administration's approach and the misnamed Inflation Reduction Act can be thought of as picking green winners in this way, as the so-called battery belt and other initiatives based on green technology formed a large part of the subsidy and investment programs. The EU voiced dissatisfaction with the scale of US green subsidies coming within the IRA, highlighting that the US has large federal firepower, and China obviously is very capable of mustering and directing government support, while the EU's fiscal situation is more limited, as its different nation states are still the main unit of taxation and spending.

Globalisation was attractive to developed countries and their voters, when they thought they were the only ones who could do high-end manufacturing, but it is getting harder to maintain this role.

As the era of globalisation accelerated beginning in the 1990s, a pattern emerged where developed country companies began to 'outsource' production which was labour intensive to developing countries, benefiting from their cheaper labour. A loose, tacit understanding was that developed countries could specialise in sectors that were more capital-intensive and/or were using more recent innovations, which supported their higher wage levels, while the developing countries got the chance to get on the bottom rung of the export-led growth ladder. At this time, all the developed countries capable of doing high-end, capital-intensive and innovative manufacturing were high-wage countries or, like South Korea, on their way to being such. This pattern was justified by the free trade ideology, which posited that trade should be free to be dictated by relative prices which would respond to international differences in wage rates, and act to arbitrate them to more equal levels, the assumption being that developing country wages would rise. The mathematically provable comparative advantage gains from trade would make the world richer as a whole, bringing growth and efficiency for all.

But China is disrupting and threatening this pattern by having super-aggressive industrial policies seeking to find a place within many sectors formerly naturally assumed to be the domain of high-wage countries. One study concludes that China can be identified as the, or a, leader in 37 of 40 areas identified as areas of key technology, and most visibly it seems China is set to become the leading vehicle producer in the 21st century.[1] In past years, China's government had a prominent 'Made in China 2025' policy, which had an emphasis on areas like aerospace, robotics, and electric vehicles. One suspects they dropped publicly mentioning this policy around 2018 to reduce the concerns of other countries, rather than actually dropping the policy direction itself.[2] The longer-term economic questions triggered by China's success through its industrial policy playbook are challenging. The most ardent free traders believe it is rational to still stick to free trade and free market rules, even if your competitors are winning the competition game by using unfair advantages like subsidies and other government supports. They would argue that it's better to just enjoy the cheaper consumer prices, so if another country wants to subsidise your consumers' consumption, let them, and the market mechanisms will automatically find another way for your country to pay its way in the world. But many who see their employment prospects harmed disagree. As the familiar debates highlight, it is a wrench to try to encourage middle-aged manufacturing workers used to good wages to move into being service sector workers or gig economy hustlers.

A weakness of the positive picture of globalisation and the division of labour it suggests is that rich developed countries need to keep discovering new and/or more advanced economic activities in order to still have sectors to employ their workers in, after the steady flow of sectors being ceded to lower-wage countries has left. But is it really safe to assume the patterns of technology and innovation, combined with changing consumer tastes and business needs, will really continue to provide new avenues of economic activities that create the businesses and jobs required? In past decades, new technology and innovation has indeed spurred whole new sectors of employment, but it is always dangerous to assume the future is a continuation of past trends. Like most things in economics, the relationship could be more like a curve, meaning fewer and fewer new opportunities to create new jobs in high numbers. This point chimes with points made by Robert J. Gordon in his book 'The Rise and Fall of American Growth', where he posits that a period of exceptional growth has ended, and one should not expect modern economies to live up to trends in those times. With manufacturing expertise in China catching up developed countries, even those who innovate new opportunities might prefer to manufacture in China, leaving developed countries out of the lucrative early productivity and consumer-driven sweet spot.

"Keynes' signal contribution to saving capitalism was recognizing that it required national economic management. Capitalism worked only one country at a time, and economic interactions among countries had to be regulated to ensure they did not impinge too much on domestic social and political bargains." 'Straight Talk on Trade' Dani Rodrik p49

One apt analogy could be drawn with children's clothes in a large family with not much money, where they hand down clothes. The eldest child gets new, larger clothes every year, letting all the siblings hand down their clothes as they grow in a chain pattern. But if the eldest child does not get new clothes, instead of handing down their old clothes, the family may go to further lengths to keep the clothes where they are, which in this analogy equates to industrial and protectionist policies. If technology is creating fewer new jobs than before, or if China is cornering key areas providing possible new technology jobs for developed countries, the tacit chain pattern breaks down, and full-on globalisation with outsourcing, etc., no longer looks so harmonious and desirable to developed countries. Instead, the trading environment moves from harmonious trading to a fight over who gets to produce and sell the high-end goods and services. This arguably illustrates the changing tone of trade policy over the last decade.

The harmony and sustainability of globalisation basically rests on how well it suits the developed countries that have the power to set the rules and the consumer markets upon which the system depends. As long as developed countries can maintain low unemployment, reasonable wages, and their electorates are happy, then the greater consumer purchasing power coming from outsourcing, etc., will be supported. But if the jobs outsourced in the manufacturing sector are not replaced by good jobs in other new areas, then discontent threatens the status quo. It is not just that developed countries 'like' to have an advantage in high-tech sectors; it is that they 'have to' have it in order to maintain employment at the affluent wage levels for their population. Technology and innovation are the rich country's only ace card, and the only thing that replenishes the global economic system from the top. The economic theory to support globalisation would assume that it would be impossible for US workers to be perpetually without work, because in theory, the cheaper imports are only cheaper due to the higher value of the dollar, and the value of the dollar is only high relative to other currencies because other countries have a high demand for dollars to buy things from the US. But the complication is that what if the factors maintaining the high demand for the dollar were tech businesses or things like oil exports which had few employees, or US brands, or other countries just wanting US financial assets instead of reciprocal exports?

People and societies have an uncanny knack of believing what they want to believe. One of the premises of Karl Marx's work was the idea that the political and economic views of a person were dictated to a large degree, whether consciously or subconsciously, by their own economic self-interest and by their own place within the class or production system. Over the last sixty years, rich countries have done well out of the free trade and globalisation ideology, but if the system creates too much unemployment or inequality, voters and subsequently politicians will start to question and challenge the beliefs and policy directions of the system. In the recent past, when the free-market system has not worked for other more unfortunate countries, Western societies have been willing to swallow various spurious reasons for someone else's misfortune. In contrast, when their own situation becomes unacceptable, they will not swallow ideological economic dogma which suggests waiting for some future improvement, but instead demand political change now, even if they don't fully understand the implications, and care little about going against the advice of the majority of economists.

"trade technocracy has instead opened the door to populists and demagogues on trade. It has allowed trade in general to come under attack instead of the specific problematic flows"
'Straight Talk on Trade' Dani Rodrik p233

Employing industrial or protectionist policies to help national inequality or so-called 'left behind' regions has become an important debate in the US and other developed countries. As China and a few other smaller exporters have become good at manufacturing an ever-wider range of goods, the regions in the US that once specialised in manufacturing have experienced a sharp reduction in manufacturing jobs. The perception that China has not played by the rules in terms of its subsidisation of its manufacturers gives the US government a legitimate excuse to put tariffs on Chinese imports and therefore aim to provide a lifeline to domestic manufacturers. Also, the workers in China seem to be kept on lower wages compared to other industrialising countries, with studies showing Chinese workers only gaining 40% of their theoretical value added, compared to a global norm of nearer 70%.[3]

"when globalization collides with domestic politics, the smart money bets on the home team." 'Straight Talk on Trade' Dani Rodrik p72

"The technological 'arms race' between backward countries trying to acquire advanced foreign knowledge and the advanced countries trying to prevent its outflow has always been at the heart of the game of economic development." 'Bad Samaritans' Ha Joon Chang p127

"The apparently effortless technological supremacy Americans assume as a birthright is significantly based on

special, transient circumstances." 'Three Billion New Capitalists' Clyde Prestowitz p112

"The danger is not that countries with money will purchase American companies (directly or through their national companies)—which they will—and make off with the 'shareholder value,' which they won't. The real danger has to do with where the spillovers of innovation go. Recall that innovation has over the past fifty years provided more than half of all real economic growth in the United States and that almost all of these benefits from invention and innovation spilled outside the innovating company." 'The End of Influence' Cohen & Delong p124

The car industry is a key desirable economic sector that developed countries will be unwilling to lose to China, illustrating why protectionism is back on the political agenda.

Even supposedly free-market Western economies have always been apt to treat some sectors and products as special, and have always been willing to break with free-market ideals if their own producers are under threat in these special sectors. The car industry is the clearest example, where US and European governments have often been willing to go that extra mile in subsidies, bailout rescue plans, protecting tariffs, and imposing import quotas, to keep them in business. Cars are a key sector because they have that magic combination of being both a product that requires very complex and capital-intensive production, and also something that rich people of all countries spend on, or a large scale. They therefore represent a massive ecosystem of complex factories and parts suppliers, which provide relatively well-paid jobs and often export revenue on top. Also, likewise in recent decades, microprocessor chips, now found in most electronic goods, have also become a focus of special contention and concern, as the COVID times and the concern over China highlight Western supply chain vulnerabilities of this key input product.

Other countries are set a challenge by China: in which desirable sectors do they concede and let China become the main supplier, and in what sectors do they abandon free market and free trade ideals and counter industrial and protectionist policies with their own policies? Germany is an extreme example, which has done very well in the past few decades from exporting high-end manufacturing goods, including cars, train parts, and manufacturing machinery, into China. These companies have also had to engage in many partnerships, where German companies have set up factories in China. But China's aggressive industrial policies mean that the know-how and technology transfer which was ceded by these partnerships have helped China on the journey to becoming able to produce its own high-end manufactured goods, with Chinese companies requiring less and less of the input from the German companies who assisted in the process. For example, Germany's car companies, with VW being the most significant, achieved a small portion of China's car market, but now this share is already shrinking. VW sells 38% of its cars to China, with Mercedes and BMW also having a third of their sales in China. But the key factor is that these are all fuel-driven cars, while China's own producers are doing well in the electric car market.[4] Sales of luxury German cars are falling, with Porsche closing some of its dealerships, rather than expanding as would be expected in a country getting richer.

"But the combined German market share in China has gone down from 25 per cent in 2017 to 17 per cent in 2022. Not a single German car is in the Chinese top ten anymore"
'Kaput' Wolfgang Munchau p65-6

Will Germany feel happy to see its exports of cars to China shrinking, either as a share of the market or even in outright sales, while China seeks to export cheap electric vehicles into the EU? Does the rest of the world stand by and let China dominate these flagship and most obvious green sectors, like electric cars, batteries, and solar panels? Companies in other countries are learning that this lumbering beast of an industrial policy and production and export machine, might crush you if you are trying to feed on the big and obvious sectors it has targeted. Will other developed countries be willing to let go of these big, obvious world markets and instead see a role as diversifying or migrating their more nimble, innovative, and market-responsive manufacturing expertise into other smaller, niche sectors, where the powerful but ungainly manufacturing giant China will pass by? In other words, will the West bow down and concede to China's massive scale, subsidies, and focus in these key large sectors while seeking to pay their way in the world by producing other specialist high-skill goods and services? I think in the example of solar panels it has already happened, but what will happen in other areas like vehicles? Below Keynes, at the height of the pressures Britain was facing due to its high gold standard exchange rate and tariffs abroad, expressed some realist truth about the conditional or partial support for free trade that most politicians actually show with their actions, despite any rhetoric to the contrary. The examples he gives of cars, steel, and farming are still hot trade topics nearly a century later!

*I am no longer a free trader—and I believe that practically no-one else is—in the old sense of the term to the extent of believing in a very high degree of national specialisation and in abandoning any industry which is unable for the time being to hold its own....I believe, for example, that this country is in the long run reasonably adapted for, and ought always to have, a motor industry, a steel industry, a farming industry. If it is proved to me that in present circumstances and at present wages these industries cannot live, then I am in favour of protecting them. But a real free trader would answer without hesitation—let them go. For some months past I have been trying to find some responsible person who was in this good old traditional sense a free trader but I have not found one. Persons calling themselves free traders nearly always retort either that the industries can thrive without a duty or even that a duty would be actually injurious to them. But such answer has nothing whatever to do with free trade—a real free trader would not even want to know the answer to these questions...*July 1930, Keynes letter to Prime Minister, Collected Writings vol XX p379-380*

Already before the latest Trump tariffs, the Biden administration had enacted a 100% tariff on EVs from China, even before Chinese EVs were imported on a large scale. The EU has imposed their own tariff, although they are at least attempting to show WTO-type legitimisation for their actions. This legitimisation has been achieved by conducting a formal 'anti-subsidy investigation', to calculate the alleged subsidies China's different carmakers benefit from and then applying different tariff rates accordingly. This currently results in a 45.3% total tariff for the Chinese car company deemed to have been subsidised the most, with the other two main brands having 28.8% and 27% total tariffs applied. But one suspects that even if no subsidy could be alleged, and China could just outcompete the EU producers based on lower wages and other costs, and larger economies of scale, the EU would still end up putting tariffs on. The WTO-type legitimation using subsidy estimates is a nice badge to have, but another justification would have been found. No doubt there would come into play a bit of 'we will do whatever it takes' if certain domestic car brands were threatened, whatever the loss of free trader credentials or criticism from the already waning influence of the WTO. This 'whatever it takes' action might secure a good share of domestic markets for their home producers, but trying to use subsidies to compete in the wider markets of the rest of the world will probably not be economically viable if China is in the same market offering far lower prices. So while today the norm is, for example, for the African middle class to be driving German and Japanese and Korean cars, in the future they will probably be Chinese electric cars. China already makes a third of the world's cars and already has the capacity to make half. There are more people working at the BYD R&D department than work for the whole of Tesla.

For many countries, the rising trade threat of China provides both the motivation and justification to use ever more tariffs and subsidies. The increase of competitively priced Chinese goods challenging existing supply chains and domestic producers provides the motivation, and the use of heavy subsidies and the lack of reciprocal trade by China provides the justification. The implication of tariffs is that, unless the exporter takes all the hit, imported goods become more expensive. The aim is for domestically produced goods to become more attractive, and therefore implying private business will find it more worthwhile to invest. Note this is, all other things being equal, the government taking money out of the economy in a tax, and the cost-of-living pressure for consumers going up. The X factor variable in this thinking is to what extent those exporting goods into, for example, the US, and being subjected to the Trump tariffs, will absorb the cost of the tariff themselves to maintain market share? This alludes to the optimistic claims in the second Trump campaign that tariffs effectively paid by China's exporters to the US could bring in tax dollars, which could allow lower income tax rates.

Time will tell what actually happens to prices and trade patterns, but it's worth noting that these two outcomes from tariffs present a trade-off with one another. A certain sector of goods being put under a tariff can raise tariff revenue in so far as the exporters manage to absorb the tariff and still compete in the US consumer market. Or, alternatively, the tariff can stop the goods coming in by allowing domestic US producers to gain market share. But the important point is that these things are mutually exclusive, in that to the degree to which the domestic production is increased, the tariff tax on imports is therefore not collected, as the imports have not come in. Likewise, if tariffs are used as a tool to create instant leverage to bring supposedly misbehaving countries like China to the negotiating table, then the implication is that these tariffs will be reduced in the future. So likewise, the tariff as a temporary negotiating tool, or as a permanent incentive for long-term domestic business investment, are also mutually exclusive aims, as a tariff rate going up and down to motivate negotiation is not a stable business environment to motivate investment.

Subsidies, in contrast, are the government putting money into the economy and giving private business a starting boost or a helping hand, in theory to hopefully become competitive in world markets. The implicit effect on an economy, again all other things being equal, is to increase government spending and perhaps therefore borrowing. Subsidies do not raise the cost of living like tariffs by immediately raising the prices of goods. But the downside in this case is the worsening fiscal and borrowing situation if the government is giving out subsidies, which must mean higher taxes or more borrowing, and the more indirect inflationary pressures that this expanded government stimulus will bring. Therefore, this in theory will arguably also in the end increase the cost of living in these more indirect ways, like through higher interest rates to control inflation.

In the case of both tariffs and subsidies, they are government interventions, and the government has to decide how to direct and manage them. For tariffs though, the decisions are usually a response to high import levels having displaced goods previously supplied with domestic production, and therefore action is already partially suggested by trade flows. Tariffs are also usually tied to some interpretation that explicit or implicit rules have been broken by a trade competitor in order to explain why a foreign country is able to displace domestic producers, and therefore give the action justification and legitimacy. Although a justification for tariffs based on an accusation of rules broken can be subjective and open to debate, the volumes of imports that triggered the action are tangible, and the money collected by the tariff and the new market prices of the tariffed goods are also very tangible. If subsidies can be called trying to 'pick winners' in an uncertain world, then tariffs can be thought of as trying to pick or identify present or recent losers in the trade game. These sectors are where a country's companies used to do OK, but now are suffering from competition. The subsequent insinuation is that, from a critical perspective, tariffs can be thought of as an attempt to wind back time or an attempt to reverse the creative destruction of economic progress. But this slight assumes that the source of the new competition has won the trade by only legitimate means, which brings us back to accusations made regarding China's economic system.

In contrast, subsidies tend to be inherently more future-looking, and proactive rather than responsive. Subsidies and other government support, although having similar aims to tariffs, require governments to make more subjective predictions regarding what sectors it is worthwhile to support, based perhaps a bit on current consumption and trade data, but based probably more on opinions about future possibilities for new products which consumers in the home country and abroad will want in the future. This, of course, is the 'picking winners' weakness noted by those who are against subsidies.

China seemed to be the ideal outsourcing manufacturing location for Apple who got rich: But Apple might turn out to have been lured into the biggest example of technology transfer in history.

In his recent, highly recommended, eye-opening book 'Apple in China: The Capture of the World's Greatest Company', author Patrick McGee tells the whole fascinating story of Apple, and in the latter half of the book, focuses on how Apple has become so dependent on China for its manufacturing. The smartphone is, of course, the most iconic and consequential consumer product of this century, and Apple has become the world's most valuable company by producing the most innovative and desirable brand. Although iPhone sales peaked in 2015, Apple has managed to maintain high retail prices and reduce its production costs.[5] The whole story portrayed in the page-turner book reveals the multiple issues and challenges Apple has gone through, many of which intersect with the issues of outsourcing, trade, and technology transfer discussed within this essay.

Apple gradually found that China offered the best place to manufacture its labour-intensive products, and a large part of that was the standard outsourcing incentive of cheaper labour costs, which conforms to the standard comparative advantage rule. But besides the usual factor of developing country wage levels, the Chinese government created further favourable conditions for labour supply, through helping to ship in internal migrant labour,[6] allowing and even helping build huge self-contained campuses with dormitories, banning unionisation and worker rights pressure groups, having a lax attitude to excessive overtime working in peak demand periods, and repressing any negative press (not always successfully) regarding unhappy workers.[7] Apple does not open its own factories, but uses subcontractors, with Taiwanese Foxconn being the key player among many. Apple now estimates it employs in China, 3 million workers in manufacturing, and another 1.8million in app development.[8] Despite some recent efforts at diversification, 90 percent of Apple's production still occurs in China.[9]

" "Nobody in the West can ever understand how China [attracts] so many factories. It's literally—you're given land. They'll build the infrastructure for you. If you expect the buildings, they'll build them for you. They'll help you with your interprovince migration. If there's not enough labour in the zone they want you to go on, they'll get you the people and they'll bear that cost. " " 'Apple in China' Patrick McGee p214

"In September 2024, some 1,500 Samsung workers in India formed a union and went on strike, demanding higher wages. Their story was broadcast worldwide by the BBC, in effect shaming the Korean company into prioritizing compliance. In China, such dissent would receive no media support and be crushed." 'Apple in China' Patrick McGee p369

"Apple has sleepwalked into a new reality: China has become the only place in the world where it could possibly build hundreds of millions of iPhones each year, and an ever-increasing number of the companies involved are Chinese rather than Taiwanese, American, or global multinationals." 'Apple in China' Patrick McGee p328

The production of Apple's iconic and uncompromising 'design-first culture' products demands intense attention to detail, and bespoke manufacturing processes and plant. McGee's book drives home the sheer technological and problem-solving input that went into the different steps in the different technological advancements. Apple had a constant flow of teams of its best engineers and experts travelling to China, to set up and train production lines and bespoke machine operations, with there being around 1000 Apple engineers there in 2013, for example.[10] Because

Apple's products were so ambitious and cutting edge, with an uncompromising commitment to design, quality, and desirability, many of the production issues and demands were new challenges and extremely tough to meet. It is possible to claim that making the early ground-breaking iPhones on the scale required was one of the biggest manufacturing challenges the world has ever seen. The investment Apple has made into China is massive, estimated as \$55bn per year by 2015.[11] Although Apple does not own factories in China, it spent billions on specialist machines, owning \$7.3bn worth of machines in China in 2012, worth more than all its buildings and stores in the US, and rising even higher to \$13.3bn by 2018.[12] Also, on top of this at some points contractors and the Chinese authorities were even willing to subsidize the costs of the specialist machinery required. Apple found the contractors and local Chinese authorities very willing to help in any way to achieve its extremely demanding production goals quickly and efficiently.

"It wasn't uncommon for a newly minted engineer at Apple to fly to China within days of getting the job—often for the first time in their life—and come back shocked at the level of labour intensity and the tight control the company wielded over dozens of factories ... "After I started, I called my family and was like, 'Oh my god, this is ridiculous! Apple doesn't do anything the way I learned it.'" "'Apple in China' Patrick McGee p176

"They were handcrafting luxury phones but doing it in mass-market quantities. ... To reach that quality, Apple has to come up with new processes to make the phones; but until Apple chose a new design these processes wouldn't exist.

95

So it had to work far more intimately with suppliers. ... He uses an analogy from the automotive world: it's one thing for Volkswagen or GM to make 10 million cars a year; what Apple was doing was akin to making 10 million Ferraris a year." 'Apple in China' Patrick McGee p268

Apple's products are among the most high-tech mass-produced products in the world, and hence its production techniques and processes must also be the most cutting-edge. The scale of Apple's operations is illustrated by the fact that by 2015, Apple was embedding its engineers when required into 1600 Chinese factories.[13] The combination of this level of complexity with such high volumes means, like the example given of cars above, it inevitably created clusters of expertise and excellence, which could then provide the opportunity for cross-fertilization to other business opportunities. Just like the heterodox economists such as Erik Reinert and Ha-Joon Chang emphasize, path-dependent opportunities in economic development thrive off the existence of such cutting-edge manufacturing happening in a locality, being called positive externalities in economists' jargon. Because Apple's products were improving and innovating so quickly, Apple found that its rapidly changing production habits were creating large swings in demand for the factories supplying it, which was making dependent businesses go bust on a regular basis. This was causing Apple bad headlines in China and bad will from suppliers. In response, Apple encouraged suppliers to have other customers so as not to be so reliant on Apple.[14] But this inherently helped technology transfer patterns accelerate, the result being Chinese companies like Huawei, for example, have made surprising leaps forward in the technological quality of their products, as the manufacturing capability trained by the best Apple engineers is easily available to other companies. By 2014, Chinese companies supplied 74 percent of their own massive smartphone market.[15]

"It wasn't really "outsourcing" in the normal sense—that would imply it was sending blueprints to companies capable of taking the orders and executing. Instead, Apple was routinely sending its top engineers, designers, procurement specialists, and lawyers from the United States into hundreds of factories across the country, where they'd import machinery, train armies of workers, coordinate the delivery of intermediate goods, and scrutinize suppliers to ensure compliance." 'Apple in China' Patrick McGee p5

"So under Tim Cook's leadership, Apple had built redundancy into the supply chain, teaching multiple vendors how to do the same thing to mitigate risks of overdependence. ... Given Apple's scale and manufacturing concentration, the result of this strategy is that Apple spawned the formation of major industrial clusters in which engineers from Cupertino would teach multiple factories ..." 'Apple in China' Patrick McGee p268-9

"the local supplier would work for soul-crushingly low margins with the understanding that it could profit from the incredible volumes Apple demanded. It could also use these new skills to win orders from other clients, charging them more for similar work. ... The message was: We won't pay much, but the experience will be invaluable." 'Apple in China' Patrick McGee p269-70

"But over time, Cook's team grew to understand that the innovations it came up with would be mimicked in China,

usually within a year. This was simply the cost of doing business there." 'Apple in China' Patrick McGee p271

"Apple, by contrast, created intimate connections to make the supplier work well beyond their own perceived capabilities, and then actively encouraged them to thrive independently so they wouldn't be overly exposed. As Apple's engineers spent thousands of hours codeveloping processes with local suppliers, they were modeling a domineering attention to detail and teaching problem-solving techniques with specialized machinery and different materials. "I don't remember, ever, a strategic withholding of information," says a former Apple industrial designer. "All we cared about was making the most immaculate thing ... We were inventing every day." 'Apple in China' Patrick McGee p273

"... Apple hired out of MIT, Caltech, and Stanford, or poached from Tesla, Dell, and Motorola, ... Apple could send a calibre of talent to China—what one Apple veteran calls "an influx of the smartest of the smart people"—that no government program ever could." 'Apple in China' Patrick McGee p282

China has allowed Apple to make billions of profits while millions of Chinese workers work incredibly hard at repetitive tasks for modest wages, and the contractors are held to very tight margins. The conventional wisdom towards Apple's business model has been that of the typical outsourcing narrative, where developing country labour helps Western consumers and Western companies get a great deal. But now McGee's book presents a different technology transfer narrative regarding Apple in China. In the book, some Apple suppliers were noted as saying that Apple was difficult to work for and drove a very hard bargain, but the suppliers and contractors wanted the opportunity to have Apple engineers and experts bring their people and factories up to a high level of competency. The volume of Apple's super high-tech training and investment into China was and is very high, constituting a massive boost to China's manufacturing capabilities. The eye-opening tech standard of the phones and EVs, etc, coming out of Chinese companies recently, can arguably to a large extent be traced back to the technology transfer bestowed by the thousands of weeks Apple engineers spent in Chinese factories. Apple is now trying to diversify its manufacturing, but China now offers by far the best complete ecosystem of manufacturing capabilities and capacities in the world. Whatever innovations Apple's leading designers desire, China is becoming the best and easiest place to have those designs turned into production capacity at the required scale. China is no longer a cheap labour destination where things only get assembled, but the best all-around high-tech manufacturing ecosystem.

"The layperson often believes Foxconn could just open a factory in a different country; but the Foxconn hubs in China are surrounded by hundreds of sub-suppliers all ready to compete for the next major order. ... "There's all these subcontracted, speciality niche firms, and nowhere else does that exist," " 'Apple in China' Patrick McGee p369

Two decades ago, Apple executives, like everyone else, assumed that China was going to be tempted into becoming a free market capitalist country, and more like Western countries in its economics and politics. But, especially since President Xi took over, China is not moving in this direction, and Apple has and is still playing a major role in helping China advance in economic and military capability. Gradually, through being eager to offer better deals, including offering to finance expensive equipment, more of the subcontractors Apple works with in China have become Chinese-owned companies, rather than, for example, Taiwanese like Foxconn. Rather than being the standard type of profit-maximizing companies focused only on maintaining a good business relationship with their customer, Apple, these Chinese contractors come with other implicit obligations and aspirations tied in with wider China industrial policy goals and the interests of the CCP.[16] This so-called 'Red Supply Chain' has also become more prevalent in Apple's supply chain by strategically purchasing existing subcontractor companies, and luring away key personnel with attractive offers.[17]

"Whereas smartphone rivals like Samsung could bolt a bunch of off-the-shelf components together and make a handset, Apple's strategy required it to become ever more wedded to the industrial clusters forming around its production. As more of that work took place in China, with no other nation developing the same skills, Apple was growing dependent on the very capabilities it had created." 'Apple in China' Patrick McGee p176

"The point, however, isn't to condemn [CEO] Cook or Apple. It's to convey the predicament they're in. ... "You can say that we read them wrong, that we misunderstood China. But Jack Ma read China wrong, too ...." Xi changed the game completely." 'Apple in China' Patrick McGee p361

Throughout its recent past, many times Apple has compromised its moral positions and indirectly assisted the authoritarian Chinese government in repressing the capabilities for free speech and political dissent. Apple has helped the government limit its Chinese customers' access to the world internet and controversial information, and helped limit the capabilities for political activism.[18] China has demanded that iPhone customer data be housed in Chinese data centres, and Apple has given in, and also assisted in the banning of thousands of apps like The New York Times, encrypted messaging tools like WhatsApp, and virtual private networks.[19]

Apple went to great lengths starting nearly a decade ago to convince the Chinese government that Apple was good for China, and it worked.[20] Apple executives had meetings with top Chinese officials where they emphasized the massive investments and technology boost Apple had and was going to make into China, to try to maintain its favourable treatment. Apple's investment and technology transfer have obviously matched with China's government's industrial policy goals, but what happens when Apple wants to diversify away from China? Chinese authorities have already tried to hinder efforts at increasing smartphone production in India by creating restrictions on certain worker visas to India and equipment exports to India relating to the smartphone industry. This suggests China does not want to see a technology transfer flow in the opposite direction.[21] As Apple tries to become less dependent on China, there may come a point where the Chinese government turns on Apple, with all the many dark arts and levers at its disposal, which China's government uniquely has.[22] And that is not to mention the issue of President Xi's hints that he wants to take Taiwan back into China. Apple relies very heavily on TSMC, the world-leading Taiwanese chip producer.[23] Apple is still a US company, and the military assurances given to Taiwan by the US pose a risk for Apple's relationship with the Chinese government. When and while the Chinese government deems Apple as making a positive contribution to its economic goals, Apple is supported. But the massive injection of manufacturing know-how Apple has historically provided China will not ensure lasting cooperative relations forever, or the continuing high sales of its products in China forever. Once the government feels that its own producers are capable enough to take over the high-tech markets without Apple's knowledge input, Apple's usefulness will be finished. As McGee's book implies, rather than Apple being the super profitable, exploitative, outsourcing capitalist Western company, it might soon look like Apple is the one that has been used by China.[24]

"It's not merely that Apple has exploited Chinese workers, it's that Beijing has allowed Apple to exploit its workers, so that China can in turn exploit Apple. ... China brilliantly played its long-term interests against Apple's short-term needs." 'Apple in China' Patrick McGee p6-7

Export-led growth based on increasing manufacturing competence has been the main route to economic development, but now China and de-industrialisation trends are making this harder.

One of my favourite anecdotes regarding international trade reveals something very fundamental about the essential fragility and confused nature of our behaviour regarding its rules and theories. It concerns the history of Ecuador in the 1990s, and I read about it in one of my favourite books, 'How Rich Countries Got Rich, And Why Poor Countries Stay

Poor' by Erik Reinert p60-1. Like a lot of developing countries, and especially South American developing countries, Ecuador in the 1990s still had the remnants of protectionist, infant industry-type policies in its economy. The policies kept a certain amount of industrial activity within the country protected from imports from larger foreign companies. But at the same time, the infant industry policies had not nurtured the South Korea or Japan-style transformation into creating world-class exporters. In the 1990s high point of free trade ideology and hubris, the international experts pressured Ecuador to wipe away its scattering of protectionist policies, and instead focus on being more free market-oriented. The advice was that the country should let its economy focus on things it naturally had a comparative advantage in. So instead of trying to protect infant manufacturing enterprises which had not transformed into mature competitive companies, in Ecuador's case one area it had a natural comparative advantage was exporting bananas.

So promises were made and pressure applied. The government of Ecuador duly cut its protectionist policies, and a section of the economy involved in manufacturing withered away, as the small domestic manufacturers could not compete with cheaper imports. Ecuador also duly ramped up its banana production and exports. But then the contrarian and what Reinert calls the "assumption juggling" reaction of other countries undermined the direction Ecuador was being encouraged to move in. When Ecuador was doing what it was advised to do by the international economic establishment, this meant its bananas were entering foreign markets in higher volumes. It had a comparative advantage in producing bananas after all, so this was the natural result to be expected. But when the increasing exports started to affect other producer countries that had links to, or were in the EU, such as the Caribbean islands with French and British connections, Greece, and the Canary Islands, the EU decided to put tariffs on Ecuador's bananas to repair the damage. So, in this rather schizophrenic way from the vantage point of Ecuador, the developed countries were quick to pressure and advise Ecuador to cease its infant industry industrial protections and focus on its natural comparative advantage. But when the potency of this natural comparative advantage caused actual disruption to existing trade patterns, one hand of the developed world was quite happy to play by different rules and ignore the free-market ideology that its other hand had been pressing upon and preaching to developing countries. Although the ups and downs of trade relationships and Ecuador's banana trade may have made this story ancient history by now, the anecdote of what happened in those years does highlight the inconsistent and schizophrenic attitudes to trade rules which have been and are all too typical.

The infant industry, industrial policy and export-led growth routes to economic development, although providing a mixed bag of success and failure, can still be argued to be the common thread in the majority of development success stories, including, of course, China. But, as Dani Rodrik effectively argues, the opportunities and potential for developing countries to climb up using this manufacturing exports ladder are diminishing. The weight of the trade agreements of the last few decades has squeezed out the possibility of taking the first import substitution step in developing simple manufactures for home consumption, let alone creating a growth cluster suitable for competitive exporting.[25] Incumbent players in manufacturing exports, led by China, have already established a strong lead in a broad swath of manufacturing, and unlike in previous generations, have still kept relatively low wages. Just as the concepts of clusters and path-dependent development are so central to the industrial policy school of thought, so the other side of the same coin is that countries that have created a head start for themselves in manufacturing capabilities provide a massive barrier facing those other poorer countries that want to join the manufacturing and export-led growth playbook. As Paul Collier explains in his book, 'The Bottom Billion', the differential between the wages in the developed countries and outsourcing countries was 40 times larger before outsourcing became a trend in the 1990s.[25] Furthermore, thanks to ever-developing technology, new sectors of manufacturing cannot absorb unskilled labour productively on such a scale as in the past, as modern automated production requires more skilled entrants.[27] Another factor is the pattern that consumer spending on services is growing faster than on manufactured goods in developed economies.

"When will the boat come around again? That is, when will the bottom billion [poorest people in the world] *actually be able to break into global markets? The automatic processes of the global economy will eventually bring the boat back around. But the bottom billion will have to wait a long time until development in Asia creates a wage gap with the bottom billion similar to the massive gap that prevailed between Asia and the rich world around 1980."* 'The Bottom Billion' Paul Collier p86

"On the trade front, competition from China and other successful exporters combined with the reduction in

protection levels means that few poor countries now have the opportunity to develop simple manufactures for home consumption. The room for import-substitution was squeezed out." 'Straight Talk on Trade' Dani Rodrik p91

"Globally, the principle of fairness should include leeway for poorer countries to grow their economies. That means not saddling them with restrictive rules on intellectual property, industrial policies, capital-account regulations, and investor rights, as current regional trade agreements typically do." 'Straight Talk on Trade' Dani Rodrik p235

From the perspective of being a citizen in a country that has not yet managed to develop economically, these are depressing points to accept. If you are not a citizen in one of these countries, stop and think how it would feel to see little hope of your country getting more affluent. The poorest countries today can be argued to be stuck in a kind of reservoir of potential factory labour, waiting for the present incumbents of export-led growth sectors to become too rich to be competitive in world markets. This is happening slowly, with even China's slow rise in wage rates motivating some Chinese companies to outsource themselves. But China is not about to outsource in sectors with the best prospects for synergies or productivity explosions, so one should expect the sectors it is outsourcing will be deliberately pretty basic. Passing on the development baton is therefore a slow process, and a person in a very poor country might think it intolerably slow. Various rules in the WTO have allowed some concessions to least developed countries, but the trade concessions remain theoretical if a country has no industry with which to benefit from them.

"high growth requires something on top: production-oriented policies that stimulate ongoing structural change and foster employment in new economic activities— manufacturing industries in particular. Growth that relies on capital inflows or commodity booms tends to be short-lived. Real growth requires devising the system of carrots and sticks that coax the private sector to invest in new industries that they would not have otherwise, and doing so with minimal corruption and adequate competence. If history is a guide, the range of countries that are able to pull this off will remain narrow." 'Straight Talk on Trade' Dani Rodrik p241-2

One line of thought is that, as services are playing an ever-bigger role in economies, the new generation of developing countries could miss out, or leapfrog over, the usual manufacturing step in economic development and go straight to specialising in services. India, the Philippines, and other countries with good English language abilities have specialised in services in this way. But the weakness with this approach is that sectors which specialise in exporting services abroad require educated workers, while in contrast manufacturing (at least the old sort) could absorb masses of less educated workers straight from other sectors like agriculture. Also, services, although they can be good export earners, inherently do not possess the same magic ability to enjoy productivity gains that manufacturing does. Manufacturing accounts for a high proportion of R&D investment in successful countries, as this is where the best innovations and productivity gains can be achieved. Automated machines and processes can mean more and more units per worker, but call centres and accountancy operatives still require one worker per call or per contract.[28]

"It is not implausible that the East Asian tiger economies will be the last countries to ever experience industrialization in the manner to which economic history has accustomed us. ... bad news for equality." 'Straight Talk on Trade' Dani Rodrik p91

"Agglomeration mechanisms are one way to explain the observed unevenness in the spatial distribution of activity and income. ... The approach predicts that development is not a process of steady convergence of poor countries to rich ones, but instead the rapid transition of selected countries from the poor club to the rich club." 'Economic development 2.2: The formation of new centres' Henderson, Shalizi, Venables.

"When Asia broke into these markets it did not have to compete with established low-cost producers, because it was the first on the block." 'The Bottom Billion' Paul Collier p167

China is likely to dominate certain economic sectors where its industrial policies are effective, and yet the flaws of its economic system mean it will still fall short of true economic success.

It may seem contradictory to suggest both that China's industrial policy is frighteningly effective at conquering foreign markets in high-end manufacturing, but then at the same time hold negative expectations about China's economic future overall. But I believe that both things can indeed be true at the same time. Yes, China's potent industrial policy means that in specific areas where it has picked winners, as discussed, like in electric vehicles, batteries, and solar panels, it will significantly dominate world markets. But, like the dynamic affecting many developing countries, just because China has a fraction of its population employed in world-beating companies does not make up for the inefficiency of the bulk of the population and the economy they work within. Like a point that Dani Rodrik makes below, having a few companies and sectors at the cutting edge of innovation and efficiency grabs the economic and business headlines, but what matters for the whole economy is the average productivity overall for all the workers and businesses, not just the showcase sectors. The inefficiencies of being an economy with heavy bureaucratic and political involvement will still be putting costly inefficiencies on everyday businesses. Having prices which are severely distorted by so much government intervention will still be imposing a massive, accumulative drag on the efficiency of the Chinese economy, pulling it well below its potential. Having inefficient businesses propped up by government subsidy due to political incentives is still harming national efficiency. The problem for the rest of the world is that even with only a few per cent of its population employed in world-beating companies in key sectors, that is still millions of workers and billions of dollars' worth of competition-crushing export goods every year. So, China could conceivably crush the world economically in key sectors, yet still be at risk of imploding politically if its growth and unemployment levels do not remain bearable.

"In Latin America, economy-wide productivity has stagnated despite significant innovation in the best-managed firms and vanguard sectors. The apparent paradox is resolved by noting that rapid productivity growth in the

pockets of innovation has been undone by workers moving from the more productive to the less productive parts of the economy—a phenomenon that my co-authors and I have called "growth-reducing structural change." " 'Straight Talk on Trade' Dani Rodrik p154

In recent years, the weaknesses of being a planned economy with complex and distorted economic and power structures have come home to roost for China, as the building spree which resulted in gross overinvestment and overbuilding, has led to a property price slump. Also, the debt incurred from the portion of infrastructure that is not worthwhile has to have had a negative impact. The model of having local politicians being motivated to achieve growth in their region at any price, plus the motivations of getting rich off the planning fees and inevitable kickbacks off construction activity on their patch, meant building was not motivated by genuine need and prospective return on investment capital, but by the benefits of having building activity for its own sake. The property boom was put into overdrive by the Chinese government's response to the 2008 financial crisis and recession in the West, where domestic economic activity had to fill the gap of falling exports to the West. Some estimates put average Chinese house prices at their peak compared to average earnings at ratios of more than 20 to 1, which is far more than noted during other countries' property bubbles. But now that the bloated building sector has busted, China will arguably be forced to return its focus to exports to try to maintain reasonable growth and unemployment rates for its massive population.

Some economists argue that, like Japan after its big property crash around 1990, China is entering a balance sheet recession, which can only mean more pressure to push out cheap exports to the rest of the world to plug the gaps in its economy and pay back its internal debts. Cheap exports for a country with such pervasive industrial policies and subsidies could likely be classed as 'dumping' by its trading partners, meaning the trade frictions between China and the rest of the world are only going to get worse in the coming years. Note that the fractious and negative trade relations of the 1930s as discussed above, had their root cause partly in Germany being put under harsh pressure to gain export revenues at any price to pay its WWI reparations. Although China has not got the formal international pressures placed upon it which Germany had, China's domestic pressures to compensate for a bursting property sector and the pressure to maintain growing economic prosperity for its massive population and find jobs for its graduates every year, will nonetheless add to the intensity with which it competes in world trade. So it's likely that China will be a disruptive factor, making the weather in world trade over the coming decades, as it relentlessly pushes out its market-disrupting exports.

CHAPTER FOUR

Other more General Points Regarding the Rules and Characteristics of Today's International Trade.

A harmonious trading system has reciprocity and symmetry, while distortions leading to surpluses and deficits cause disharmony: Look at the trade statistics and not the rhetoric.

Reciprocity is one of the most useful words and concepts in discussions of international trade. So many negative situations have arisen regarding trade throughout history because countries did and do not appreciate that trade relationships need to contain some reciprocity to maintain goodwill on both sides. Likewise, many policies or national ambitions in areas of trade can be revealed as flawed if they contain non-reciprocal relationships. Any trade policy should recognise the implications of any distortions it creates, both on a country level and an international level. As Keynes was expert and devastatingly effective at explaining, the subject of trade relations and economic balances contains many rigid mathematical economic relationships, otherwise known as identities, which will always have the last word if pitted against political hubris or short-term or selfish thinking. If the distortions created by a country's policies and export and import activity cause issues for other countries, sooner or later the other countries will act to repair any negative distortion they are experiencing.

"It is no longer possible for Americans to continue to think of ourselves just as consumers and not as producers." 'No Trade is Free' Robert Lighthizer

"At the time of Smoot-Hawley [1930s] we ran an unreasonable trade surplus that we wished to maintain. We now run a damaging deficit that the whole world knows we must correct." 'America's Growing Trade Deficit Is Selling The Nation Out From Under Us'. Warren Buffett (see below Chapter 5)

"For decades, the United States has been the world's indispensable spender. Countries whose residents save too much and spend too little have consistently been accommodated by Americans who borrow to spend more than they earn." 'Trade Wars are Class Wars' Klein & Pettis p174

It is a technical impossibility for many countries all at once to be the lead exporter in any one desirable sector of production or services, just as it is a technical impossibility for all countries in the same year in sum to be exporting more than they import. Every exporter needs an importer. All trade policies must be able to fit into a theoretical trading world where all other countries are either employing the same approach or happy to assume the mirror image of any trading asymmetry your country's policy is generating. One country stating it wants to dominate trade in most of the desirable economic sectors of that period can be interpreted as quite an aggressive stance. Does that country want to claim the cream of all the benefits of the best advances in technological production for itself? Or is it willing to merely have its share or specific, limited specialities? The pattern of the past has been that the countries that economically developed first in Europe and North America were the only countries capable of producing in these desirable markets, with Japan and then other countries like South Korea joining them. Although run through with instances of industrial policies, tariffs, and other trade rules and policies representing the protection of incumbent interests, the underlying pretence of there being free markets, where the best and most innovative and efficient producers succeeded, just about survived in that period.

As discussed, protectionist policies can be interpreted as a country being selfish and cheating on the ideal rules for international trade harmony, which provide the best results for the whole or common good. The most desirable trade policies are those that seek to reduce imbalances and distortions in trading relationships, rather than those that blatantly seek advantage for one's own country. A pure system of free trade, in theory, would have few imbalances and distortions because currency exchange values and prices would automatically adjust to create equilibrium in imports and exports in, and between, all countries. But once one accepts there are imbalances and distortions created by other countries, then industrial and protectionist policies which clearly and sensibly aim only to address those imbalances and distortions can have a level of legitimacy and justification which more blatantly selfish policies do not have. Trading partners are entitled to get annoyed at a country doing old-fashioned mercantilist industrial policy when it already has a trade surplus, but a country with a persistent trade deficit is more entitled to be taking action. As in other areas of life, aggressive actions taken in self-defence or in response to another's unfair actions are inherently less contentious.

Although China often produces statements in support of free trade and warning against having a trade war, the realities of its trade numbers reveal a gap between imports and exports which do not match this rhetoric. It's one area where talk is definitely cheap, and actions, and the statistics which back them up, really do speak louder than words. As discussed, the particularities of China's economic and political system present many opaque and informal obstacles for foreign country imports into China, and the actual trade statistics show that actual economic conditions must be hindering free trade, even if those impediments are not obvious or provable. Whatever the rhetoric, the real proof is in the trade statistics, and it is the statistics that should legitimise, or not, interventionist trade policies. In the past, of course, China's non-reciprocated trade surplus was used to buy U.S. Treasury bills. More recently, the surplus has gone into other assets like private equities, with US tech stocks and even gold showing surges in demand thanks to China. Another side point is that Germany in recent decades has also been an aggressive trade surplus country, and the issues of the imbalances within the EU which came to a head over a decade ago, are another example of surpluses and imbalances leading to further frictions and pressures for other countries.

"Systematic transfers of wealth from Chinese workers to Chinese elites distort the Chinese economy by strangling purchasing power and subsidizing production at the expense of consumption. That in turn, distorts the global economy by creating gluts of manufactured goods." 'Trade Wars are Class Wars' Klien & Pettis p3

"places that squeezed consumption relative to production simply forced production to fall relative to consumption elsewhere. This had significant consequences for trade."
'Trade Wars are Class Wars' Klien & Pettis p83

Some economists who are strongly against protectionist policies claim that they are the wrong answer to solving a large trade deficit. They believe instead that trade deficits can be viewed as the product of a country's low net saving rate, as predicted by working through the strict accounting-type theoretical identity that describes all countries' finances.[1] This is the big national income identity central to macroeconomics, which is kind of a double-entry bookkeeping representation of the flows of money within any economy, which always by definition balances, subject to a margin of error. The identity asserts that net national savings (savings minus borrowings) minus investment (which is an important variable factor representing employing resources but not for regular direct and present consumption) must/will equal net national exports (exports minus imports). The identity represents in accounting language the intuitive point that if a country is consuming more from other countries than it is producing for other countries, it must, on net, be borrowing from/selling assets to, other countries to pay for this extra consumption. (If you want to further understand this concept, it's easy to look it up online, and also see Warren Buffett's essay in chapter 5.) National net savings include all private saving and borrowing activity, and also importantly the identity includes government borrowing. Therefore, with this line of thinking, the free trade economists conclude that a country should get its domestic house in order by reducing net borrowing, i.e., most importantly reducing its yearly government spending deficits, rather than trying to seek answers by launching protectionist trade policies on its trading partners.

But I would argue that although the identity is of course valid by definition, it is possible to think about the causations and possible solutions being the other way around. The implicit suggestion in the free market economists' arguments is that the government of a country should respond to trade deficits by introducing policies that increase net savings. These are basically tightening policies, such as increasing taxes, reducing government expenditure, and raising base interest rates to change private saving and borrowing habits. But I would argue that the tightness or looseness of fiscal and monetary policies in a modern democratic economy is strongly dictated by other factors, and no government or central bank could tighten fiscal or monetary policy based only on negative trade or net savings numbers. Instead, monetary and fiscal policy stances adhere strictly to optimizing between the two boundaries of maximizing economic growth on one side, and preventing inflation on the other side. The base interest rates for any modern Western country are always and at all times set at a level targeted between these two big boundaries. Interest rates are as low as possible to achieve maximum growth, but are raised when the economy is overheating, which is usually interpreted to be only when general price inflation appears.

This assertion about interest rates is illustrated by the example of the decade and a half after the 2008 financial crisis, when the US and other Western countries maintained historically very abnormally low interest rates, despite criticism from some economists regarding the distorting effects this had on the property and investment markets. The iron unspoken rule of setting monetary and fiscal policies to achieve maximum growth was followed. There were at that time no signs of inflation, and most developed economies were still experiencing sluggish economic conditions. So even if this meant extreme monetary conditions, that is what the monetary conditions had to be. Again, the fixed and overriding goal of economic policy in a democratic country is that the economy not be in a recession, so monetary policy and fiscal policy will keep adjusting in response to political pressure until this is the case. I would argue that to claim there is a choice to use these policy areas for other lesser objectives, like increasing net savings rates or reducing the trade deficit, is to underestimate the focused pressures on governments and central banks to maximise or protect economic activity.

An interesting aside is to note that to have your monetary and fiscal policies dictated by the need to reduce a trade deficit and or improve net savings levels is (and in history was) answered by a gold standard type system. In the Gold Standard system, its rigidities meant the requirement to maintain a gold price fix or gold reserves automatically dictated when austerity or tightening policies were required, even if the wider conditions in your country were already recessionary. This of course was part of the dynamic of the Great Depression, where countries already in recessionary conditions but with trade deficits, were forced by the policy mechanisms and conventions of the gold standard to try to create greater austerity and frugality in their own country, to choke off imports and make exports more competitive, and therefore win trade (and hence gold) off each other. Although attractive to certain thinkers who value economic discipline and living within your means, the reality is that modern electorates would not put up with monetary and fiscal policies that kept an economy in austerity or recessionary conditions to serve other, lesser objectives, like savings rates or trade deficits. Although free market economists are quick to make the link between protectionism and the 1930s, the notion that a country should respond to challenging international trading conditions and trade deficits with ultra-disciplined domestic austerity policies is also kind of repeating one of the other mistakes of the Great Depression, which Keynes famously noted.

To illustrate the argument that trading conditions could cause negative net saving rates rather than the other way around, I want to explore an extreme thought experiment. Imagine if tomorrow some of the factories in the world outside the US were destroyed and prohibited, say in all of the countries of South or Latin America, and those countries were forced back to only producing agricultural goods and commodities, and the only manufactured goods they could consume would be exports from the US. Some free market economists might still assume that the net savings rate of the US should not be affected, as they would argue the savings rate is dictated by the domestic desire of US consumers to consume versus the desire to save, and the government's political desire to be popular by spending more than they tax. But if the goods from US factories became suddenly extremely desirable to South American countries, the profits and wages of US manufacturers would rise quickly. Also, US consumers would be buying more from domestic producers rather than buying imports. The extra income of the business owners and workers would mean they had more money than what they had previously gotten used to, and would be in a position to save more and borrow less.

Imagine a US where the demand for its goods from abroad was very high. Prices of manufacturing inputs and labour would rise due to demand outstripping supply. The government and the Fed would soon feel like it was experiencing an overheating economy, and so would raise interest rates to cool the economy and prevent high inflation. The raised interest rates, as the mechanism of that policy lever intends, would reduce private borrowing and increase private savings. Also, the tax take of the government would jump up, and the spending on benefits to the poor would reduce as more better-paid jobs became available. The government finances would look rosy, and the government would see little need to borrow to juice the growth rates in the economy. The government would find that yearly government surpluses were easily achieved, and beneficial in cooling off some of the excess demand in the economy. Therefore, in this thought experiment, a trade shock has directly influenced the domestic net savings rate. It is therefore not much of a leap to go from arguing that US exports being in high demand would improve net savings, to then argue the counter, which is that cheap imports and exports being not as attractive can lead to strongly negative domestic net savings, as lax monetary and fiscal policies are pursued in order to maintain a thriving domestic economy in a world with challenging trading conditions.

So a fixed factor in the picture surrounding this debate, I would argue, is that the fiscal and especially monetary policies of modern Western governments always track towards a sweet spot between inflationary and recessionary conditions. Therefore, if the trade relations of the US are sucking demand out of the economy and putting pressure on domestic businesses, then monetary policy will be loosened until borrowing (net negative savings) rises enough to make up for the recessionary effect of the lack of demand for US producers. Rather than claiming trade deficits are caused by negative savings rates, it would therefore be possible to claim that fiscal and monetary policy react to counter the pressures international trade relations are putting on a country, and that lax or stimulative policies are inevitable to increase borrowing rates to take up the slack. As the thought experiment illustrated, a country with strong demands for its exports would tend to have more restrictive or tight monetary conditions in order to cool the economy, and would expect to be reducing its government borrowing. Another scenario where a country was experiencing balanced or symmetrical trade relations would tend to have neutral fiscal and monetary policies, neither lax nor tightening. Finally, a country in a world where the major trading partner is running a $1tn yearly trade surplus, which represents 4 percent of total world trade! would arguably tend to be needing to run lax or perpetually stimulating monetary and fiscal policies, to try to maintain acceptable economic activity levels and prevent recessionary conditions.

The claim of the free trade economists is true that savings levels and trade deficits are connected, but the causation direction is where opinions differ. As is typical in economics, the nature of the identity is agreed upon by all, and the debate is in the arguments regarding which factors are fixed versus which factors are dependent, and therefore which way the causation relationships flow. Although there is merit in the opposite opinion, I would argue it comes back to the theme of this section: that in trade, reciprocity and symmetry are desirable, while surpluses and deficits have negative effects, both obvious and less obvious. Free market economist are right that the issue is not bilateral deficits, and many protectionist measures fail in their intended effects due to trade being diverted or replaced by a third country. Free trade economists are also correct in asserting that to desire a balanced trading relationship with any one country is a false aim, as trade by its nature is fungible and apt to divert and find its natural level through a different route, like flowing water. For example, it would not matter if the US had a worrying trade deficit with China, if China at the same time also had its own trade deficit with a third country, and that third country had a surplus with China and a deficit with the US, which would repair the US position and balance out everything globally. But this is not the case, and so that still leaves the big fact of China's massive trade surplus as a negative presence in the international economy. Just like Germany needing to have a trade surplus at any price to pay its reparations was a negative factor on world trading conditions during the Great Depression, so China running a massive trade surplus to make up for its own lack of consumer spending is a big distortion, rippling out to affect the rest of the world in a negative way.

Hayek made the strongest arguments regarding the dangers of governments making 'arbitrary' decisions to protect certain groups against the distribution mechanisms of free markets.

The arguments that gave me a true understanding of the word 'arbitrary' in the sense used in this essay, I found in the book 'Law, Legislation and Liberty'. The author, right-wing economist F. A. Hayek is one of the most influential economic thinkers of all time. At one point in that book, Hayek defines 'arbitrary' as: "action determined by a particular will unrestrained by a general rule", which gets right to the heart of the subject of this essay. p351. Hayek argues that some of the most important facets of successful free market economies came about through trial and error, and are actually poorly understood and appreciated. Hayek also stresses that in a democracy, often politicians are prone to try to respond to the demands and lobbying of interest groups by creating policies that reward them at the greater expense to the rest of the population of consumers or taxpayers. Because politicians have these powers to reward special interests, the competitive political bargaining process means that even worthy politicians can be sucked into a race to the bottom. They are tempted to make compromises to buy off minority interest groups in a way inherently against the long-term economic interest of the whole country. Hayek argued that the entrenched interest groups that are experiencing a reduction in their position due to adverse competition are the most likely to angle for such political protection, often employing the vacuous social justice concepts to help their case. Any negative feedback the spontaneous order is generating in the interest of progress (i.e., making the candle maker poorer when the light bulb is invented), the government is requested to halt. Hayek argues that this trend inhibits the smooth functioning of the searching and dynamic knowledge processing capabilities of the 'Great Society', and is a step towards what he calls the hideous monstrosity of a totalitarian system, where the political system dictates everything.

If an economy has too many of these sub-optimal policies, cumulatively they mean an economy is less efficient and will experience slower growth. Growth, after all, usually comes from innovations and disruptive factors that create more consumption with the same inputs, and this can include using trade as an innovation to exchange more for less. To combat this slide into arbitrary, harmful policies that politicians get tempted into due to the competitive political process, Hayek argued it is better to tie the hands of politicians in this area. He argued that rather than the modern trend towards seeing a political majority as representing a right to change all laws, some economic laws which enshrine the attributes of what he calls the 'Great Society', should be protected from even a government or administration with a clear majority. This is like the idea of having a constitution, which needs far more than a simple majority before a single government or administration can change it. If all politicians were able to defend themselves against the demands of interest groups by stating they did not have the powers to make 'arbitrary' policies favouring any one group, then the whole political system would become healthier. Obviously, this thinking speaks to those who believe that President Trump should not be able to change trade tariffs so freely and so arbitrarily by himself. Trump's tariffs do seem the very definition of arbitrary and are favouring specific interest groups like steelworkers and manufacturing workers. But his supporters would argue that the tariffs are part of a wider political ideology and direction for the country, which he campaigned on and therefore has a mandate to deliver, and the tariffs are not just about winning transactional votes from specific workers. There will be very strong beliefs on both sides of this debate.

"... socialism is based throughout on the atrocious idea that political power ought to determine the material position of the different individuals and groups ... It was the great merit of the market order ... that it deprived everyone of such

power which can be used only in arbitrary fashion." Law, Legislation and Liberty, F.A. Hayek p260

"We can prevent government from serving special interests only by depriving it of the power to use coercion in doing so, ... the only defence that a politician has against such pressure is to point to an established principle which prevents him from complying and which he cannot alter." Law, Legislation and Liberty, F.A. Hayek p359

"To ask for protection against being displaced from a position one has long enjoyed, by others who are now favoured by new circumstances, means to deny to them the chances to which one's own present position is due." Law, Legislation and Liberty, F.A. Hayek p256-7

Industrial and protectionist policies, with their arbitrary rules and judgments, require high-quality, benevolent government personnel and increase the scope for corruption.

One big advantage of free trade policies, compared to protectionist and industrial policies, is their clarity of direction versus the subjectivity, arbitrariness and contentiousness of the latter. In some ways, a country having a free trade policy in its trading arrangements is an aim to have an absence of policies and an absence of government interference. For a country to practise free trade and free markets, it needs to focus only on reducing the distortions affecting the theoretical true market prices within its economy, so as to allow prices to efficiently allocate resources between different goods and services and so also let the free market decide what goods and services that country should export and import. The feedback loops contained in the market and trading systems need only light-touch management and to be left alone to provide the right incentives through prices for most economic decisions. In the free market model, the role of government is to create the right environment for businesses to thrive, but not to actually get involved in decisions like where to invest or what imports and exports to encourage or discourage.

In contrast, once a government steps into industrial and protectionist policies, it is immediately forced into making subjective and arbitrary decisions. On which goods should we put tariffs on imports? Which countries should we target, and by how much compared to others? Which companies or investment projects should qualify for subsidies? How do we calculate the unfair advantages China gives to its exporters to be able to make things fair for our producers? What sectors do we want to protect so that our domestic companies can create a locus of speciality and capabilities, and eventually become world-competitive? Will the policies create world-competitive companies, or will interventions be required to continue indefinitely? All these questions create winners and losers in an economy, even if the losers are spread thinly around taxpayers' funding subsidies, or consumers and/or businesses paying higher prices for goods. And because industrial and protectionist policies can create small groups who gain a lot while spreading out the costs to consumers or taxpayers more broadly, this animates economists to point out the probable slippery slope, as alluded to in the above section. The worrying trend towards inefficient behaviour is where focused interest groups who gain from protection or subsidy will fight hard through the political system to retain it forever, while the less focused consumers or taxpayers quietly get milked for a few pounds or dollars each.

The perennial weakness or danger in this dynamic is, of course, the scope industrial and protectionist policies create for politicians and bureaucrats to engage in sub-optimal political compromises at best and even corrupt practices at worst. How much will the businessman pay to lobby the politician to get their goods protected by tariffs? How much subsidy is worth giving to a company in a region with a close political battle coming up? How much tariff costs are worth imposing on the whole of the domestic economy in order to benefit the steel workers and local economies of key swing regions? Free markets and free trade provide little opportunity or scope for graft, as any extra costs imposed by corruption are in danger of making goods and services uncompetitive in lean markets. But introduce the element of non-free market advantages like tariff protection or subsidies, and now there is some fat available in the system for the unscrupulous to trim off for themselves, without killing off the golden goose of the business involved. This basic observation, that industrial policies are more conducive to corruption because they inherently involve arbitrary decisions and subjective policies and interventions, must remain central in the thoughts of anyone thinking about the future of such policies. Policy solutions that manage to have less arbitrariness and more semi-automatic or market-reliant mechanisms are therefore more desirable.

Japan and later, South Korea famously had a very competent and focused government and bureaucracy for implementing their successful industrial policies. The authorities expertly directed and coerced their key companies from protected novices into world-beating exporters who no longer needed support. However, many other developing countries, including most notably Latin American governments, which went into protectionist policies strongly a few generations ago, were far less efficient and self-disciplined in this area. Most of their protected sectors and companies never escaped a crony-filled mediocrity. In China the picture is more mixed. Yes, China's industrial policies have had a very successful impact on its growth and industrial capabilities. But at the same time, the opportunities for corruption due to China's lack of separation of powers and free press, etc., have made doing business in China full of opportunities for graft for those who can find themselves with the right political connections. But also full of unfairness and danger for businessmen, who can find their hard work taken from under them by those with better connections, or their positions threatened by false corruption charges. Read 'Red Roulette' by exiled former successful Chinese businessman Desmond Shum to appreciate these points.

"We played a similar game with a vast array of bureaucrats. Each approval was obtained through connections. Each connection meant an investment in a personal relationship, which meant an awful lot of effort and even more Moutai [alcohol]." 'Red Roulette' Desmond Shum p139

The efficiency and economies of scale in the supply chains and production processes of factories have played a large role in creating affluent countries: Protectionist trade policies can harm this.

The pros of a country doing industrial policy can be summed up as the country sacrificing its maximum present efficiency and maximum present consumption in order to achieve some kind of dynamic transformation. The country doing industrial policy is going against its natural present comparative advantage in what it imports and exports to supposedly create new clusters of expertise and capability to give them a brighter future. The concepts of comparative advantage, of course, explain the costs of preventing trade most convincingly, but it is also useful to think about the different practical factors involved in thwarting the comparative advantage ideal. There is no doubt that economic history has many examples where the industrial policy approach has provided long-term advantages for a country, which make the short-term sacrifices worthwhile. But at the same time, this does not mean that every country taking up every potential opportunity to partake in industrial policy would be a good thing. To frame the debate over industrial policy at the expense of free trade and comparative advantage, it is useful to identify specific costs in economic efficiency of such policies in order to be able to consider them sensibly and give practical examples of what these inefficiencies actually look like.

Thinking about the extreme case is useful here, as it illustrates the subtle but real costs involved. For a start, it is true to assert that factories making things on a large scale are a big part of what has improved the average standards of living over history. The combination of large investment in the automation of super productive machines, reducing labour inputs, and achieving high economies of scale provides the magic ingredient that creates affluent societies. But by definition, these factories have the biggest and best impact when they can achieve large economies of scale. Of course some products, like mainstream food items, have such a high consumption rate that it does not take that large a population for the factory to be fully utilised. But the situation is different for a factory making goods that are less frequently bought. In this case it can make a large difference whether a few competing factories serve the market of the whole trading world, or whether industrial policies have been used to forcibly plant similar factories in many different countries, thereby each time dividing the market up between more factories, and duplicating the capital spent and plant manufactured for the new factories each time. Although this explanation is necessarily imprecise, this kind of duplication cost is real and must be considered a real factor that makes the world definitively poorer if industrial policies are overdone in sectors of production with limited volume markets.

The supporters of industrial policy and infant industry arguments make some very convincing points about economic development which are strongly supported by history, and recently by the rise of China and the other specific Asian countries who did and are practising these policies. But one key weakness in the industrial policy and export-led growth school of thought relates to a systematic way of thinking about looking at trade on a global level. This is that if all countries were to follow their prescriptions to protect, subsidise, and nurture infant industries in sectors where they perceived opportunities to create maximum clusters of competencies, synergies, and spillover effects for their economies, the patterns of world production would form into a crazy situation.

The logical conclusion of this would be that every ambitious government in the world would be pushing subsidies (paid for from taxpayers' money) or saddling their consumers with higher prices thanks to tariffs in the same 'promising' sectors, which provided the same hoped-for 'good jobs'. As discussed, in present times, these could be areas of technology with a demand based on green factors, the prime example being EVs, or microprocessor chips, which are central to so many modern products. So in this thought experiment, to take the industrial policy school of thought to the logical extreme, it would lead to a world where every government of every country with any manufacturing ambitions would choose to be subsidising its own exports of solar panels, wind turbines, chips and EVs, and at the same time all these same countries would be putting up high tariffs against these same goods being imported from other countries. The consequences for market prices and trade flows are arbitrary in the extreme. By definition these sectors are high-tech, so fixed or upfront costs tend to be very high relative to marginal costs. Therefore, duplicating factories for similar products in every willing country represents a needless massive investment drain and lost economies of scale when viewed from a global perspective.

This thought experiment highlights a crucial weakness of the arbitrary nature of industrial policy and protectionist thinking when taken to its logical extreme. In such a situation, what rules (rules in both the man-made rules sense and in the rules or laws of the science of economics sense) would dictate what desirable goods and services are produced where? Would it depend on which country's government was most determined and had the deepest pockets? Imagine the outcome of such distorted markets in these sectors if everything were dictated by government intervention while efficiency and economies of scale played no role. Surely countries fighting so hard to gain a place in these sectors would mean they were producing at a loss when all wider costs were considered? As Hayek described so well in the different but similar area of talking about politicians being motivated to make arbitrary interferences in market mechanisms in order to improve illusive concepts of social justice, he argued there are no *"practical halting points"* for the socialists to settle at until the destination of complete totalitarianism is reached.[2] In other words, once you depart from the 'rules' of free trade and free markets, there is just an endless sea of arbitrary possibilities remaining to be debated over, and no rules to provide a natural, settled policy destination.

A generation ago, there were only a limited number of countries with advanced manufacturing capabilities, but now, partly thanks to outsourcing and technology transfer, there has been a step change in the proportion of the world's population with industrial capabilities and capacities, and this trend is only going in one direction. Whereas in previous times there was more likely to be room for a country to achieve its industrial policy goals, now with so many countries positioning themselves in different ways, the fact that there is no potential harmonious point at which countries can be held in a stable international relationship is more obvious. Free trade policies may have baked in previous advantages and given less opportunity for developing countries to proactively shape their economic futures, but at least the free trade ideal provided a certain limited kind of harmony and rational order, in contrast to the arbitrary, free-for-all of a world of ever more proactive industrial policies.

If a country has companies producing tradable goods that enjoy high economies of scale, this makes exporting very attractive. In other words, once the fixed cost of the plant and machinery is in place, extra units can be churned out for relatively little marginal cost compared to the prevailing selling price, so this would encourage that country to seek to expand its export markets for those goods. The factories of Britain in the times when Britain had an empire, no doubt benefited from the semi-protected markets for their goods that the empire created. Likewise, when China lures countries into its economic orbit by offering 'Belt and Road' investments and loans, implicit in the economic relationship is that more goods from Chinese factories with high economies of scale will be purchased by these developing countries. A proportion of the money from the loans China gives out will be used to buy these Chinese goods with high fixed costs but low marginal costs, and the borrowing country still has to repay the loan later, so it's a win-win. It might not always be the prime factor in decisions about loans, empires and spheres of influence, but it certainly is a factor.

As already mentioned, the environment already has a big role in industrial policy questions because the need to reduce fossil fuel consumption provides a few of the best sure-thing bets for governments if they are looking to 'pick winners' in terms of economic sectors likely to grow. The other angle on environmental issues that affect trade questions occurs when a country perceives that the difference between its own environmentally friendly policies and a perceived lower standard in another country allows the other country a competitive advantage. For example, China is responsible for half the world's coal consumption, partly for the energy it needs for the goods it exports to the rest of the world. This is contentious if competing producers in rich countries are paying higher energy bills due to policies to reduce global climate change. There is therefore a predictable call for border adjustment tariffs to compensate for this unfair advantage, but the calculations and implementation headaches involved in this kind of tariff are great. The search for suitable 'rules' in this area would involve arbitrary judgements and estimates, and seems quite a political exercise, despite the genuine economic point at its core.

CHAPTER FIVE

An Interesting Diversion: A Plan Suggested Two Decades ago by Warren Buffett for Reducing the US Trade Deficit.

This plan was detailed in an article by Warren Buffett called, *'America's Growing Trade Deficit Is Selling The Nation Out From Under Us. Here's A Way To Fix The Problem—And We Need To Do It Now.'* November 10th, 2003, Fortune Magazine (searchable online).

The plan has some desirable automatic market mechanisms, which reduces the need for arbitrary decisions from politicians and bureaucrats implicit in other protectionist approaches.

Just over two decades ago, an article was published by Warren Buffett which highlighted the negative consequences of the US continually running a yearly trade deficit, and it suggested a simple, radical and yet deceptively sophisticated solution. Buffett is very well respected for his day job as perhaps the world's most famous professional investor, but he is not a professional economist known for making trade policy suggestions. As mentioned, rules and policies for trade which contain or employ semi-automatic mechanisms, as opposed to subjective and arbitrary mechanisms, are much more desirable to have. Policies and rules which reduce the need or possibility for political tinkering and arbitrary judgments and decisions provide more certainty and stability for all concerned and also reduce the scope for politically short-sighted or even corrupt outcomes. It is mainly this point which brings me to make a positive comment in support of this deceptively simple suggestion regarding America's trade deficit. I am not saying it's definitely what the US should do, and others more qualified to answer that question may have good reasons to not like the idea or be able to identify flaws in its simplicity. But a few attributes of the plan I want to praise.

As Buffett emphasised in his article, because of the special place in the world economy of the US dollar and the US economy generally, it can be argued that the semi-automatic mechanisms (which could be thought of as a key 'rule' in the science of economics) which balance a country's economic relationship with the rest of the world is distorted for the US. The special role of the dollar as the world's favourite trading currency, and the special attractiveness of having dollar-denominated reserves like US government debt assets mean the exchange rate of the US dollar tends to be perpetually too high to balance imports and exports. As mentioned above, thanks to the iron economic mechanisms or identities which govern economic relations between countries, the other side of the coin of a country importing more than it exports is that trade partners who are in surplus acquire a slice of the assets of the deficit country each year this happens. The classic case has been the rest of the world, and most notably, China acquiring US treasury bills instead of US exports. But besides government debt, other kinds of the US's assets are being increasingly bought, with dollars other countries have gained from exporting to the US. Therefore, each year a higher proportion of US domestic assets are becoming owned by other countries.

With Warren Buffett being from the investment world, he is naturally attuned to a slow but significant trend like this, which ticks away quietly but gains momentum. The dynamics of this kind of worsening compound profligacy, which means extra consumer spending and overconsumption in the present, in return for the increase of foreign ownership of America in the future, would naturally stick out more to someone who has made a fortune from financial patience and long-term thinking. Just like Buffett has seen his own fortune rise over the decades partly through the magic of compound interest growth, and him and his partners not drawing out all of their profits, so the mirror image is this trade situation, where a slow but steady trend in foreign ownership of US assets will steadily make the US worse off. In the article he puts a lot of emphasis on this deteriorating trend, and uses a simplified allegory understandable to non-economists to illustrate it. Although it applies more fittingly to America's special situation, the thinking also applies to other rich Western countries that run persistent trade deficits. Like the US, other rich countries are also dealing with the challenges from China and others getting better and better at exporting manufactured goods, while the same countries are making it difficult for reciprocating exports into their own consumers to reach equal levels.

Buffett's deceptively simple proposal was for those who bring imports into the US to be required to cover or match the value of these imports with 'credits', which can only be created by the government awarding them to exporters, and then the exporters selling them to the importers. Similar to carbon tax quotas, the price of these credits would be dictated by supply and demand, and a market set up to allow buyers and sellers to reach a market price. With every company seeking to import into the US having to acquire these credits, which can only be created when goods are exported, it is a simple and rigidly mechanical way to bring the dollar value of exports and imports into line. The awarding of this bonus of credits to exporters would make exporting more profitable, acting like a universal subsidy on top of all export earnings, which could allow either higher returns for the exporter or lower prices for the US goods in their destination country export markets. The requirement for importers to purchase credits would act like a universal tariff for all imports, with importers knowing that importing the goods would have to make up this extra cost to be worthwhile, either through higher consumer prices or lower returns for the exporting country.

"neither protecting specific industries nor punishing specific countries nor encouraging trade wars."

"Foreigners selling to us, of course, would face tougher economics. But that's a problem they're up against no matter what trade "solution" is adopted—and make no mistake, a solution must come. (As Herb Stein said, "If something cannot go on forever, it will stop.")"

"In one way the Import Credit approach would give countries selling to us great flexibility, since the plan does not penalize any specific industry or product. In the end, the free market would determine what would be sold in the U.S. and who would sell it. The ICs would determine only the aggregate dollar volume of what was sold."

"the pain of higher prices on goods imported today dims beside the pain we will eventually suffer if we drift along and trade away ever larger portions of our country's net worth."

"I believe that ICs would produce, rather promptly, a U.S. trade equilibrium well above present export levels but below present import levels. The certificates would moderately aid all our industries in world competition, even as the free market determined which of them ultimately met the test of 'comparative advantage'."

"This plan would not be copied by nations that are net exporters, because their Import Credits would be valueless. Would major exporting countries retaliate in other ways? Would this start another Smoot-Hawley tariff war? Hardly. At the time of Smoot-Hawley [1930s] we ran an unreasonable trade surplus that we wished to maintain. We now run a damaging deficit that the whole world knows we must correct."

Buffett's writing on the subject is, like his advice on investment, well worth reading and laced with the clear-sighted common sense mixed together with iron economic rationality which he is famous for. He predicts the credits becoming worth around 10 cents for every dollar of exports or imports. He also concludes that even trading partners like China might eventually conclude it is in their best interest to import more goods from the US. The positive characteristics of this trade imbalance solution are clear. Firstly, as Buffett mentions, trading partner countries cannot be upset with its logic or mechanisms. As Buffett notes, the infamous

Smoot-Hawley tariffs of the 1930s were an attempt by the US to maintain its already large trade surplus, which created aggressively negative implications for other trading countries. In contrast, this Buffett solution is seeking only to end a distorting perpetual trade deficit, and by definition, the policy will extinguish itself before the point at which the US becomes a net exporter. If the pressure creating America's trade deficit receded, then the price of the credits would adjust down. With subsidies and tariffs, those who disagree with them point to the danger of retaliation by other countries as a reason not to employ them. But with a Buffett-type plan, the opportunity for trade partners to retaliate by doing the exact same policy could only be open to those countries that were also running a trade deficit, which inherently are not the countries causing the distortions in the world trading system. China, for example, could not employ a retaliatory Buffett-type plan because it exports far more than it imports. There would be an excess of exporters wishing to sell credits compared to a lesser number of importers needing to buy them, meaning the credits would be worthless.

The second positive attribute of this kind of plan relates to the semi-automatic nature of the way in which it would work. As mentioned, subsidies and tariffs by nature tend to require politicians to make many arbitrary decisions and judgments in their design and implementation. A key danger of sector-specific tariffs is that once applied, they inherently create an immediate interest group wishing to maintain them forever, and the tariff becomes politically impossible to remove. In contrast, the tariff-like support of the Buffett plan would melt away smoothly if it were no longer needed, and no interest group could lobby otherwise. Companies and business people could observe trends in the value of the export/import credits and have a degree of certainty about their business environment, but they could not really lobby against the changing value of the credits. So in summary, while, of course, a Buffett-type solution would involve very controversial political decisions to design and set it up, once in place, the policy has a number of market-type mechanisms which work automatically, and don't require the same degree of arbitrary tweaking and tinkering from politicians and bureaucrats.

Instead of politicians choosing which sectors or goods to subsidise or protect, the process would still be left entirely to market forces to sort out. There would be no politicians at risk of being lobbied or even corrupted by interested parties or trying to 'pick winners'. The export credits could be earned by any exporting company and could likewise be purchased by any company wishing to import any product. Therefore, although intervening on a massive scale on an overall level, the Buffett plan also maintains the desirable semi-automatic mechanisms of free market ideology at a lower level of the policy's execution. The Buffett plan does not take away from the free market price system the power to dictate what is imported and exported. Of course, these import and export markets are being 'distorted' on a major scale, which is usually the enemy of free market ideology. But the distortions would be simple and transparent and adjust in a neutral and set way the information which the price system provides, rather than overruling that price information completely.

For example, a developed country government could decide that all clothes should be produced domestically and keep raising tariffs until this happened. But this would be very economically inefficient, as the present system of exchanging clothes for other exports gets a favourable exchange on labour hours. In contrast, the benefit of a Buffett-type plan is that this kind of arbitrary policy by decree would not happen, and instead the credits would encourage exactly the right production sector, which is presently 'only just' unable to compete with imports to regain market share, and the production sector 'only just' not able to compete in foreign markets to become viable exports. In economists' language, the policy would create change only in the marginal cases, minimising inefficiencies. This is in contrast to a politician who is arbitrarily choosing a sector of production, which might be a long way from being a viable market prospect, but a useful political symbol or regional vote-winner. Arguably, the issue the Buffett plan seeks to address is that the exchange rate of the dollar is too high to balance the trade deficit, and the plan does this in a targeted and clean way. The Buffett plan as a solution has a similar effect to that of a currency devaluation, and like a currency devaluation, it has a universal effect and does not discriminate between specific goods being traded, or trade partners.

CHAPTER SIX

The Importance of Competition, the Importance of Differentiating, and Thinking about Some Utopian Ideas Regarding Rules for Trade.

It is important to differentiate between different traded goods when considering industrial or protectionist policies, including the attributes of the products, their production, and their markets.

Although the debates between free trade and industrial or protectionist policies are often framed in general and absolute terms, the specifics of different sectors producing different goods have very different qualities, which makes each case different. It is usual for an economist or politician to imply they are pro-free trade or pro-industrial/protectionist policies as a broad principle applying to all trade. But here I want to argue that differentiating between the specific markets of different goods and services allows one to have a more sophisticated and nuanced approach to these questions. Below I want to discuss four different ways of differentiating between different traded goods, which could, should, and often already do inform any country's trade policies. Besides influencing actual government interventions, some of these ways of differentiating already do dictate trade to a certain degree, as they help shape the way the costs and prices affect how the goods from different countries can compete. The four types of differentiation I have come up with are as follows:

a) **To what extent does producing the product also produce positive externalities which lead to other things, in terms of spillovers, agglomerations, clusters, and transferable skills and capabilities?**

The most significant way to differentiate between different economic activities, from the perspective of a country considering its own economic well-being and development, is to think about the spillovers and positive externalities which performing that economic activity can provide. History has shown time and time again that having companies within your own country making and selling certain goods can generate improved and transferable capabilities, agglomerations, and clusters of expertise. This is the crux of the age-old industrial policy argument, where that school of thought asserts that a country needs to be involved in producing certain goods to allow it to develop its competencies and benefit from the positive externalities which lead to more innovations, new products and opportunities. It may seem counterintuitive to claim that the most consequential aspect of participating in a desirable economic activity is something which creates benefits which often accrue outside the companies actually producing those products. But like the analogy of someone's career path, a country's economic progress is path dependent, where it's not just the immediate returns which count, but the possibilities for the future it opens up.

As mentioned above, at the pinnacle of political interest in this area are the high-end manufactured goods, which produce the most spillovers and possibilities for new innovation and capabilities in a domestic economy. These are the sectors of trade which get the most political focus, while the trade in other goods and services tick away in the background, receiving less or no interest in terms of trade policies and rules. This way of thinking about trade is found in so-called heterodox economic schools of thought and is a main point in their thinking about world economic history and how poor countries will not progress if their role is only selling commodities and agricultural goods. An important factor to remember when thinking about this point of differentiation is that it is not always the actual product sold which has to be complex, but what matters is the complexity of the most efficient production process. So, for example, even some agricultural production, producing commodities like US wheat, involves high-tech machines and equipment, while other food products, like certain fruits, might involve a lot of labour-intensive and low-tech activity.

b) **To what extent do the production processes have economies of scale, or in other words, what are the fixed versus variable or marginal costs?**

The ratio between fixed and variable costs is different for different economic activities. At one extreme, a manufactured product made in a highly mechanised factory with a great amount of machines and capital in place but with little labour, raw material, or energy costs per total unit cost would have a very high fixed cost compared to variable cost. These are terms also used in accountancy language. Alternatively, an economist might say, 'marginal cost' rather than 'variable cost', which denotes the costs in making something in terms of how much making one extra unit at the end of a day, for example, would cost for a factory. Another related economic concept is economies of scale, where production processes which have high fixed costs and low variable or marginal costs are said to have high economies of scale because producing on a large scale means more of the advantages of those low variable or marginal costs are benefited from. As the section earlier on efficiency has already alluded to, this aspect of production is relevant to international trade, because if a production process has a very high fixed cost but very low variable or marginal cost of running the process for extra units, then more trade and more specialisation can make everyone better off. Likewise, it is this factor which explains how industrial and protectionist policies can cause real economic harm, as using these policies to force domestic production could be duplicating fixed costs, creating more factories, but each with a smaller output. This will therefore swiftly reduce the economies of scale enjoyed by the previous situation and therefore reduce the efficiency of the whole world economy.

c) **How intense is the market demand, or in other words, how many millions of populations would support a typical factory?**

The factor of fixed versus variable or marginal costs above should be considered for the purposes of thinking about international trade, alongside the particular market for the product being manufactured. If a product has a very high level of demand per head of population, then trade restrictions meaning only domestic companies can supply the market will, all other things being equal, be less harmful. Ideally, for the incentives of robust competition to work their magic, a number of different companies should be competing in any one market. So if the demand for a product within one country is enough to keep, say, four competing factories running at a fullish capacity in order for them to achieve the economies of scale which creates good efficiency, then the industrial and protectionist policies will not be so inevitably harmful. But if protectionist policies mean only one or two factories are left supplying the protected domestic market, and if those factories are not operating at an efficient volume, then this would imply the policies are causing an absolute dead loss of economic costs, not to mention removing the magic competition incentives which keeps companies acting in the customer's interest. This point means it's important to differentiate between economic activities also based on, in another way of saying it, how many factories that product could support producing at an efficient scale. If a certain product or component is very specialist and not many are sold compared to the scale of production which is efficient, then going hard into industrial and protectionist policies in this sector would be a recipe for inefficient and expensive outcomes. This dynamic explains why cars are such a common target for industrial and protectionist policies. They tick the boxes of being both high-end manufacturing with loads of positive externalities mentioned above, and at the same time, every middle income and rich country has quite a high demand for them per head of population.

d) What is the volume or weight-to-value ratio of the products, which obviously dictates transport costs as a percentage of total end price?

This factor comes down to simple common-sense profitability. If manufactured goods are traded or outsourced, then the product will obviously have to be shipped to the consumer country. For example, at one extreme, the number of mobile phones able to fit in a standard shipping container must be a very large number, meaning that, because of the high value compared to volume, the transport costs as a proportion of the end price must be tiny. In contrast, bulky goods, like for example, storage boxes made from formed plastic, are quite bulky compared to their value, which is why it is a sector which survives as something still sometimes manufactured within rich countries. This also applies to the production of other bulky products like sofas and mattresses, which survive high domestic labour costs in rich countries due to the alternative of high transport costs of importing, i.e., the low number of sofas or mattresses which would fit into a shipping container. Bulky (low price per cubic meter) food staples like breakfast cereal and potatoes are also usually not imported into the UK, for example. This factor naturally shapes international trade through the normal free market mechanisms of prices and profits and should be considered when thinking about industrial and protectionist policies. A developing country seeking to create some capabilities and cluster effects in a sector which produced bulky goods like sofas or mattresses would be helped along by this transport cost factor, which acts like a natural and automatic tariff on imports, benefiting local producers.

At any one period in time, there will always be 'Prize Sector' economic activities which are extra desirable to have, and therefore trade policy surrounding these sectors will be more contentious.

Much of the discussion of trade prominent in the general media and business media always focuses on certain important sectors, like currently microprocessor chips, all types of cars, and now especially electric cars, batteries, and other green technology and green infrastructure. These are the economic activities that currently give the best positive externalities to the economy in which they are located. These externalities are the synergies, increased capabilities and capacities which create cluster-effect benefits, where having one type of manufacturing leads to further innovations and possibilities. Other special economic activities with large economies of scale and large investment requirements, like building planes, are also desirable and therefore sensitive areas for trade policies and disputes. This illustrates that, in reality, every year most governments already do differentiate to a certain extent, recognising that some sectors are especially desirable to have your own companies producing in. Even throughout the high tide of free market and free trade ideology a few decades ago, politicians encouraged by companies and business leaders instinctively continued to make exceptions for and pay special attention to these sectors, which I would call the 'Prize Sectors'.

The essence of free trade and comparative advantage theories is that they focus on the comparative market prices of different goods and services in order to dictate what goods and services are made where. The perennial counterargument, which is the industrial policy and infant industry school, seeks, in contrast, to emphasise the benefits of upgrading a country's comparative advantage in a 'dynamic' system, while free trade works on the basis only of 'present' comparative advantages being continued and sustained. The point is that the tension between these two concepts can be argued to be more relevant regarding some sectors of economic activities than others, and the special prize sectors, which many countries want to be players in, are the extreme example of sectors that can dynamically upgrade a country's capabilities and opportunities. Prize sectors are by definition experiencing evolving technologies and opportunities for innovation and productivity improvements. These innovations and advancements are good at generating new spin-off products, which turn into new, profitable business opportunities and new positive externalities of knowledge to other sectors. Therefore, every government would want this on their soil, motivating the most aggressive industrial and protectionist policies. These kinds of sectors are also the ones where intellectual property and instances of industrial espionage are most significant, and where governments are most vigilant regarding these issues.

The jealousy with which governments covet sectors like chips, EVs, and batteries contrasts with sectors that have none of the possibilities for dynamic advantages, such as producing clothes. Developed country governments are not going to the same great lengths to subsidise clothing manufacturing, for example, because the dynamic future possibilities and benefits are not there. But one revealing point is that there was a time when the production of clothing was a cutting-edge technology area, and in those times, more than 150 years ago, the governments of the countries involved were fighting to keep the best bits of production within their borders and trying to get other countries and/or colonies to limit themselves to producing the raw material inputs. This illustrates that the prize sectors change over time as technologies move from being new, high-tech, and profitable to mainstream and commodified.

A few decades ago before the economic rise of China, the tension, inevitable when many developed countries all coveted these prize sectors, was always a prominent factor of trade relations and geopolitical relationships. But a key difference was that the countries capable of partaking in these most desirable prize sectors were all fairly high-wage countries and all loosely supportive of a Western, US-led and influenced, capitalist and democratic economic system. So that, for example, when Japan, with its surge of competition-beating cars, threatened domestic US manufacturers in the 1980s, the US was able to motivate the negotiation of the Plaza Accords, plus create car import quotas for Japan to stick to, all while remaining strong geopolitical allies. Now with China and, to a lesser extent, other developing countries getting good at high-end manufacturing, the potential players in the trade game wanting a share of the prize sectors are much greater; they no longer all share economic or political values and are no longer all high-wage countries. The point is that regarding the prize sectors, deciding who made what was never truly allowed to be left to free market forces to dictate, and in the current world situation it is even harder to be able to find rules or norms to decide these issues.

Protectionist policies are rightly accused of harming economic growth, but growth is not everything, as inequality and jobs can matter more, and also growth puts more pressure on the environment.

Protectionist policies thwart the route to the maximum gains from capitalist trade, hindering the maximum economic growth and consumption a country and also the world can potentially achieve. Trade can be a magic economic tool for a developed country to exchange goods that took fewer labour hours for goods that represent many more labour hours. But if the economic growth in GDP gained is accruing only to a minority of winners in the system, and those winners are using it for excessive consumption, which harms the environment and speeds up climate change, is this economic system really doing the best for everyone? For example, if a protectionist policy reduced the income (and climate impact) of the richest consumers by a total of $2bn, but raised the income of the workers by $1bn, would that growth-destroying policy be good or bad? Notably, when countries are in difficult economic recessions or depressions, it is unemployment, hardship, and the government's ability to help those in need that are the focus, not the drop in, say, new cars on the road or the pension wealth of the very rich.[1] Growth is generally a good thing for countries, but its 'goodness' is often in the more indirect effects it has on society, such as low unemployment, a tighter labour market for those at the bottom, and more comfortable government finances allowing them to spend on positive things like healthcare, education, and helping people in need.

The argument I am making is that while the growth angle is a key one when thinking about protection, it's not everything. The capitalist system, including China's version of it, has been the main way the living standards of people have improved. But taking into account the environmental impact humans have, the inequality involved means the capitalist system and the perpetual economic growth model are far from ideal. For example, an average global economic growth of 2.8% per year would mean a doubling of world output every 26 years, which also therefore means a sixteen times bigger economy in just over a century![2] That can't happen, so a change in outlook is going to come, one way or another. The bottom line is the planet cannot afford to go through the amount of economic growth required under present patterns to allow everyone a decent, Western standard of living. In order to reduce poverty, the present system would at the same time create too many very rich people, consuming too much and harming the planet. If the aim is to increase economic growth, then capitalism and free markets are unbeatably effective. But if the aim is to improve the living standards of everyone to a comfortable minimum level without destroying the planet, then it does not look so efficient. It's a tricky, controversial, and nuanced argument to make, which most economists would be suspicious of, but I think it leaves a possible, if precarious, justification for considering protectionist or interventionist trade policies as part of a more sustainable world economy.

"as the US writer Edward Abbey once put it, 'Growth for the sake of growth is the ideology of the cancer cell'." 'The End of Capitalism' Ulrike Herrmann p73

What an ideal utopian trading system might look like, if an all-knowing economist God could create and enforce complex rules and categorisations for traded goods.

What goods and services countries import and export, by definition, dictates what they do and don't produce themselves, so therefore, to dictate the trade of an economy is an important factor in dictating the actual shape of any country's economy. After 200 years of world economic growth, the country a person is born into still dictates a large part of their economic fortune, and the contrasting fortunes of different countries can largely be attributed to the history of trade. It can be argued that the economic opportunities available, which dictate which country makes and exports what products, are a big factor in predicting the success of all countries, which is not really addressed enough when world poverty and inequality are discussed. On a world scale, governments of rich countries say good words regarding helping poor countries, and are willing to provide admirable amounts of charity and aid. But at the same time, they are also very focused on making sure their own countries get to perpetuate their favourable place in the most desirable economic activities, even though this necessarily locks out the poor countries from ever becoming affluent. This is certainly a few steps removed from actually directly taking bread out of the mouths of others, as subtle rules of the game are being followed, and therefore it allows some plausible deniability. But from 100,000 feet, this can be seen as selfish if one looks at the bigger economic picture.

"nations are forced to specialize in economic activities where there are no possibilities for innovation, only to be accused later of not innovating enough. These are countries that have specialized in being poor within the international division of labour." 'How the Rich Got Rich …'Erik Reinert p230

If one believes in the themes running through this essay, that different economic activities are the key factor in different path dependencies, which then produce different economic outcomes, then thinking radically in a utopian spirit, true equality would involve systems and dynamics that shared out those opportunities in a better way. Obviously, the factors of economic efficiency, economies of scale, and the negative effects of the duplication of investment and plant costs mentioned above, mean that any solutions have to be moderate and not excessive. But it is hard to conceive of any future that is more globally equal without sharing out these opportunities in some way. Capitalist globalisation has brought a large slice of the world population out of poverty, the biggest group recently being the Chinese, as China has become the workshop of the world. But those countries waiting for China's labour cost to motivate outsourcing their manufacturing to poorer countries have an unbearable wait, making migration look attractive to many. If there were a world government elected by a democracy in which the whole world voted, would not the majority vote for, and agitate for, a system which gave this kind of hope for better economic opportunities? But there is no world government giving poor countries such power over richer industrialised countries, and rich country' population economic advantages are safely defended by their national governments.

One starting point in seeking rules to tackle some of the controversies in international trade could be to create rules, either unilaterally or multilaterally, which allow countries to produce in desirable sectors to the same proportion as that which they consume. This approach might be especially relevant in what I have called the 'prize sectors', where many countries want to be dominant and where the benefits of having that economic activity within your country are very high. This is one response to the inherent arbitrariness of protectionist and industrial policies. It would tie the policies down to a tangible factor relating to the real economy. So, for electric vehicles for example, this could end up meaning China could export into the US only the same number or total value of electric vehicles that it imported from the US. This would imply that trade between countries capable of being in the producing game would be circumscribed, while other countries without the capability for that product would remain markets to be captured in the usual way. Another approach could follow the 'look at the trade statistics, not the rhetoric' attitude. Even those who disapprove of the first and second Trump administrations' methods and approach to changing America's trade relations have to concede that the tangible numbers representing exports versus imports, taking into account services also, support Trump agitating for change and don't support China's claim to be a model free trading country. Just as the mechanisms of the Buffett plan inherently only work for a trade-deficit country, likewise, rules regarding what countries are allowed to resort to, based on real trade data, would have some merit in being pro-equilibrium. This speaks to the original themes of Keynes' thinking and also his alternative proposals during the Bretton Woods times, where he noted the lack of means of putting pressure on trade surplus countries to move towards more balanced trading relations.

So far, this essay has stayed within the realms of past and present trade policies and rules, and fairly familiar past and present thoughts on trade. Now I want to take some of the conclusions I have reached in earlier sections and use them as a basis to be more imaginative, adventurous, and even utopian, to see where it leads. Even if utopian concepts would never survive contact with the realities of self-interested domestic political systems and the self-interested economic incentives of the people and organisations involved, thinking about what ideally a utopian international trading system could look like could help inform the smaller steps that are possible. Even if an ideal utopia is forever far off in the distance, like a lighthouse on the horizon while out at sea which never gets closer, at least it might help frame the debates and provide one option for a direction of travel in these contentious and complex waters. If nothing else, hopefully this essay has shown how and why questions around international trade are complex and multi-dimensional. There are great trade-offs at play between the ruthless but absolutely crucial efficiency of free markets and free trade, which help generate economic growth and grow the international economic pie. And then there are other factors, like improving economic development for poorer countries and maintaining a degree of equality and low unemployment in richer countries.

"The idea of a perfect society is a very old dream, as Isaiah Berlin put it; such fictions help us pay attention to the 'ills of the present' and shape our direction of political travel." 'Growth' Daniel Susskind p166 citing 'The Crooked Timber' Isaiah Berlin p20

So getting into the realms of 'playing God' and thinking about what a utopian situation for international trade would look like, a number of points have been made which should frame such an exercise. Firstly, leave some sectors to world free trade, as for countries to try to use protection on sectors with sparse demand in relation to high fixed production costs would lead to wasteful and inefficient duplication of investment and poor competition outcomes. Secondly, the economic activities which have been called the prize sectors above need countries and international organisations to recognise that everyone wants to be producing them and to try to agree on sharing, reciprocity, and reasonableness. These prize sectors have rarely been left to free trade alone to share out, and more open honesty and agreement are needed to find acceptable compromises. Poorer developing countries cannot realistically hope to get involved in these prize sectors, as the bigger players will be eagerly crowding in first. Taking these two groupings off the table, there are still many sectors or products within mainstream manufacturing with reasonably high demand, remaining available for proactive industrial and protectionist policies. These more everyday sectors of manufacturing might not be the cutting-edge, exciting prize sectors, but a country partaking in them can still benefit from the magic externalities, such as increased capabilities and cluster effects. Essentially, to have complete freedom to 'play God' and start with a blank canvas, it would be desirable for example, to spread out more geographically the capability to gain the benefits that possessing manufacturing capabilities provides.

As mentioned earlier, Friedrich List in the 19th century noted that free trade and protection are each beneficial in their own way for countries in different circumstances or different stages in their development. He noted that, of course a country with many well-developed, world-beating sectors would benefit from the larger potential markets created by free trade. But at the same time, he also argued that some countries that were trying to develop their capacities and capabilities, but not yet able to compete with the best producers in the world head-on, might benefit from protectionist infant industry policies while they improve. He also suggested creating trading blocs made up of groups of countries at the same level of development. This speaks to the points made above about some products needing a certain size or scope of market in order to create enough demand to support a number of competing companies. As a side point, this thinking provides a justification of the European Union, at least in its initial trade bloc form, before the attempts at political union became more significant and controversial. The smaller European economies benefit from a trading area of similarly developed economies, which is bigger than their nation state but still protected from world free trade with its lower wage exporters. So this approach could imply, say, a group of developing African, Asian, or Latin American countries forming their own free trade area for certain manufactured goods, with the bloc maintaining a tariff wall around the whole to encourage and support the companies within, while still exposing them to adequate competition.

Going further into this concept of countries having trading areas with gradations between domestic-only trade and world free trade, the leap toward a utopian ideal could involve different manufactured goods being officially categorised into different groups (perhaps even represented by different colour categories), with some designated as having no trading restrictions (complete international free trade), some designated as freely traded only within a larger trading bloc of similar countries with tariffs around the outside, and some further protected to be only freely traded within the nation state. These designations of traded products would reflect the differentiation points made above and reflect a balance between the power of protection to bestow the positive externalities and synergies of manufacturing within a locality versus the dangers and costs of losing the benefit of efficiencies from competition and economies of scale. The key point is that protected sectors must have the volume of demand high enough to support a number of competing companies or factories operating at a suitably efficient scale to make industrial policies and protectionist policies not harmful to competition.

As a curveball point to drop into this theoretical blue sky thinking, the handful of experiments with local currencies that have popped up and mostly not lasted in the UK are related to the ideals and concepts being chewed over here. The local currencies in Bristol, Totnes, and Brixton in London represent going even smaller than the UK nation-state in trade area granularity, and trying to encourage some goods and services to enjoy preferential local advantages over more widely traded goods and services. Other countries I am sure have seen similar experimental local currency projects. One would conclude these projects are motivated by a desire to push against a perceived race to the bottom, globalised commercial world, and create more healthy and cohesive local communities. The experiments have produced mixed results, with most projects ending, and one practitioner I viewed noting that the trend towards a cashless society was not helping. Like I suspect many others, I would sympathise with the values and intentions of such experiments, but personally I am not convinced by the practicalities of such projects, and a sceptic could note the worrying potential for bypassing the national tax collection systems and other government relationships, such as means testing benefits.

Back to the ideas above, and the first thing to understand is that the devil is in the detail, as modern production patterns are rarely like the famous original Henry Ford Model T factory, where every part of a product is made from raw materials on one site. Attempting to categorise the finished products and their components in modern manufacturing would turn this simplistic notion of differentiation into a practical administrative headache. One's all-knowing God of choice would therefore be required not just to design and achieve the agreement between countries of such a utopian system, but also to achieve agreement in working out and formalising the ground-level practicalities of such concepts to be applied to the web of modern production patterns and supply chains. At every turn there would be arbitrary decisions to be agreed upon and enforced, where there is no clear-cut one answer nor authoritative rules to defer to. At the same time, for these decisions there would be many interest groups, like businessmen, worker unions, and local politicians, arguing for judgments to suit their case and protect their corner of livelihood, in conflict with the interests of others or the whole community of taxpayers or consumers. Thinking about the difficulty of trying to agree upon such subjective and arbitrary concepts and policies with idealistic goals, one is reminded of Oscar Wilde's alleged quip: "The trouble with socialism is that it takes up too many evenings!" The scope for debate and disagreement is endless.

"Rules are a device for coping with our constitutional ignorance. There would be no need for rules among omniscient people who were in agreement on the relative importance of all the different ends." Law, Legislation and Liberty' F. A. Hayek p176

One danger is to fall into the worst kind of import substitution policies in the Latin American style, which led mainly to rent-seeking cronyism and interest group capture, with average or poor-quality products and little competitive pressures to motivate world-class exporting. Free trade supporters are right to note the way protectionist policies often become unduly difficult to remove once enacted, as interest groups are created and arise to fight to maintain the support in place. Thinking about the vulnerabilities to political and interest group distortion, and the complications and decisions involved in creating and managing such an arbitrary system in our complex world, reveals why I have firmly presented these ideas within a utopian light. Again, this highlights a merit of free trade, in that the policies to enact free trade mostly imply an absence of government interference and distortion. In any country with any level of development in any time period, anyone could more or less agree on how to proceed with a free trade-based trade policy. But move into the realms of these protectionist concepts, and there would be endless variations and flavours of policies from which to pick and agree on. The different interest groups and the usual changes in political leadership add to the difficulty in picking out and settling upon one arbitrary approach among many. This line of thought highlights how much credit the institutions of countries like Japan, South Korea, and even China deserve for successfully thinking through an industrial policy approach and sticking with it for long enough to see it pay off.

I have tried to highlight that differentiating between the attributes of different traded goods could help to shape possible policy approaches to share our economic development opportunities. But I have also emphasised how problematic and arbitrary any ideal theoretical solution might be in practice, thanks mainly to the selfishness of human nature. Capitalism and free markets are such a successful set of economic organising principles, mainly because it allows for, can withstand, and even harnesses, human self-interest and greed. The reality of human frailty might mean that an ideal utopian technical answer to greater equality through trade is difficult to achieve. Being a very

162

poor developing country has been very hard for decades, and the rich world has arguably, to a certain extent, been willing to fudge over the awkward reality of this through unrealistic platitudes and economic narratives that imply patiently waiting for an improvement in circumstances. But recently being a rich country has also become harder in the trading world, and the difference is that the democratically empowered and entitled populations of rich countries will not patiently accept any negative consequences of an economic system or ideology, but instead will agitate for change, even if they are not sure where that change will lead. Whatever else is uncertain, one certainty is that the rise in the capability of China's thousands of factories containing millions of workers is triggering a massive shock wave of disruption and reaction across the world of economics and subsequently, therefore, politics.

POSTSCRIPT
Trump II

The second Trump administration is going hard into using tariffs, creating much uncertainty for business, losing the moral high ground, and in danger of making the US look just as bad as China.

I started writing this essay in early 2024, and as I am trying to complete it in mid-2025, President Trump is putting trade policy in the spotlight, and it's a bit of a moving target to comment on. Throughout Trump's presidential campaign in 2024, he mentioned his love of tariffs regularly, and a few months after taking office, he went big into proposing putting up tariffs on all countries. The severity of the tariffs proposed was intended to be linked to the trade relationship each country had with the US, with those exporting to the US more than they imported being stung with higher tariffs. The actions of putting these tariffs on, and then the later retaliations and retreats, reveal more than anything the arbitrariness possible in these kinds of policies, as argued in this essay. Hayek's definition of 'arbitrary' in the context of politicians tinkering with economic rules and laws is very apt: "action determined by a particular will unrestrained by a general rule". 'Law, Legislation and Liberty' Hayek p351. What can be more arbitrary than one man putting tariffs for different countries up and down at his whim, with only flimsy reference to general rules or economic theory or the realities of trade numbers?

The other thing highlighted is the conflict or cross purposes of the motives suggested for the tariff policy, also mentioned earlier in this essay and even by Keynes himself. Firstly, for tariffs to be used as leverage for negotiation and later reduced as part of a trade deal, they inherently cannot also provide stable incentives for domestic businesses to invest in replacing imports, as businesses would want the tariffs to be permanent and predictable. The lurching tariffs swinging up and down mean businesses and companies struggle with the uncertainty of not knowing what the tariffs will be in a few months, if they commit to plans or finance an import journey across the ocean. Also, tariffs can provide revenue from the foreign imports coming in, or tariffs can move production to domestic companies, but these things are mutually exclusive. By definition, the imports that are replaced with domestically produced goods cannot generate tariff tax income.

Although not a focus to begin with, inevitably the tariff relationship with China has become central, and as I write, the situation is very volatile and uncertain. In recent years the Chinese economy has revealed itself to be not as invincible as formerly thought by many, and tariffs might hurt more now than they did in the better times when their property market was still booming. But on the other hand, a further factor is that China has, in the intervening period since the first Trump administration, been ramping up its exports to other developing countries, and the US is now a much smaller share of its exports, from 26% down to 13%. The level of China's trade surplus in recent years has grown to over $1tn per year, which is about the equivalent of 4% of total world trade, highlighting its pattern of having too small a share of its economic output benefiting its working class, as China is more than ever, producing far more than it consumes.

China's large trade surplus emphasises that it is still a very controversial trading player, breaking the first rule of harmonious trade relations, which is reciprocity. But the irony is that Trump's style and grandstanding rhetoric make the US look like the culprit to those who do not understand the actual fundamentals and numbers. The Chinese have already tried to use the controversy generated by President Trump to paint themselves as the good guys and the defenders of free trade, when the previous sections of this essay should emphasise that this is not the case at all. There might, in Trump's second term, have been better prospects for 'issue-based coalitions' regarding trade, made up of other developed countries and putting pressure on China to be a fairer player, especially as China's rising trade surplus disrupts all other developed domestic manufacturing sectors. But Trump's rhetoric-driven style is not conducive to maintaining such collaborative and careful relationships, and he wants to act unilaterally. Once again, it seems the possibility of strengthening the global 'liberal understanding' and shared common good economic values is not going to be a priority, as Trump sees everything through his 'America First' lens.

Earlier in the section about the 1930s, I noted that rules can be drawn from Keynes' expansive writing from that time on the subject of tariffs and protection. A central takeaway is that tariffs are a tool or weapon, and like weapons they are not completely good or bad in themselves, but it depends on the circumstances and motives for which they are employed. Tariffs used in self-defence for a country with a damaging trade deficit, thanks partly to a trading partner with problematic economic tactics, can be justified. But tariffs used as economic stimulus for a country without a trade deficit, and/or as an easier alternative to other stimulative or job-creating policies, or for taxation, is destructive to the common good and triggers the game theory dynamics also discussed earlier. The Trump administration can certainly claim that the trade deficit of the US might justify its actions, but the Trump administration seems to be straying into also using tariffs for reasons other than the self-defence of trade deficit reduction. If President Trump and those around him start emphasising raising tariff revenue, or using tariffs as arbitrary bullying leverage in unrelated areas, or implying they are part of a geopolitical, ideological attack on China specifically, then the narrow legitimisation Keynes implied tariffs had at that specific point in British history is lost.

The point made earlier that a Buffett-type export credit plan would maintain the precision and efficiency of using free market prices to dictate what was imported and exported, and automatically tip the balance on what was only just currently marginally unprofitable to produce, is also highlighted by the contrast of Trump's recent arbitrary tariff action and threats. US financial markets are reacting with fear at the prospect of US companies being forced to 'reshore' specific examples of manufacturing at massive extra costs to avoid excessive tariffs. These are not the marginal products that need only a small incentive to be viable, but products way down the viability list for domestic reshoring. This extreme interventionism is the equivalent of throwing cash on a bonfire to economists, as large comparative advantage trade benefits from cheaper labour costs are swung into reverse, and US companies will be forced to offer high wages to entice US workers into repetitive assembly line jobs.

Whatever the outcome after this turmoil has settled down, I think Trump's actions will mark a permanent paradigm shift towards tariffs being higher and more prominent in the trade relations of the US, and soon other developed countries also. If China does not change its ways and continues presenting the rest of the world with its mix of aggressive trade surpluses, high subsidies, and frighteningly fast catch-up in key prize sectors of developed country production, then developed countries will respond. The style and the uncertainty Trump's policies have generated will be condemned, but I think the policy direction will not be substantially reversed by Trump's successors. I believe the call will be to do tariff policies better and more carefully, but to still do them as long as there are trade deficits and imbalances, and threats to certain domestic 'prize sectors' of production. For example, when it comes to the possibility of the West losing a chunk of its car industry, I believe countries 'will do whatever it takes' to maintain the current share of these industries in domestic markets, and free trade ideology and WTO commitments will matter little. As the section on Apple above illustrates, outsourcing the manufacturing of cutting-edge products like iPhones is changing the balance of economic capabilities between the US and China, and this, helped by that eye-opening book, will not go unnoticed by those with a 'Make America Great Again' mindset.

Just like the change in direction towards domestic free market policies and away from government interventionist policies in the Reagan era is often cited as a wider turning point in economic history, so I believe the current move to tariffs will mark the messy start of a future of more protectionist and managed trade relations in the US and other developed countries, as technology transfer becomes more of an issue. But hopefully things will get more settled, predictable, and collaborative. And hopefully politicians and economists will begin to find and create better and less arbitrary 'rules' and norms for their policies.

Notes

Chapter One

1 Paul Tucker, 'Global Discord' p111
2 Dani Rodrik, 'Straight Talk on Trade' p229
3 Petros C. Movroidis & Andre Sapir, 'China and the WTO' p75
4 Erik Reinert, 'How Rich Countries Got Rich, and Why the Poor Countries Stay Poor' p4
5 Rodrik p152-3

Chapter Two

1 Petros C. Movroidis & Andre Sapir, 'China and the WTO' p142
2 Movroidis & Sapir p128
3 Movroidis & Sapir p134-5
4 Robert Lighthizer, 'No Trade is Free' p313
5 Lighthizer p317
6 Movroidis & Sapir p40
7 Movroidis & Sapir p103
8 Movroidis & Sapir p68
9 Movroidis & Sapir p199
10 Movroidis & Sapir p113-5
11 Movroidis & Sapir p183
12 Movroidis & Sapir p42
13 Lighthizer p119
14 Movroidis & Sapir p198
15 Movroidis & Sapir p46, p91
16 Movroidis & Sapir p47 p176-7
17 Movroidis & Sapir p46-8
18 Movroidis & Sapir p145-6

19 Movroidis & Sapir p188
20 Movroidis & Sapir p50-2
21 Lighthizer p64
22 Lighthizer p65 p79
23 Lighthizer p81
24 Lighthizer p210
25 Lighthizer p64
26 Movroidis & Sapir p56
27 Lighthizer p276
28 Lighthizer p152
29 Lighthizer p153-4
30 Lighthizer p211
31 Lighthizer p208
32 Lighthizer p235
33 Movroidis & Sapir p59, p212
34 C. Fred Bergsten 'The United States vs China' p193
35 Bergsten p286
36 Movroidis & Sapir p148
37 Lighthizer p202
38 Jake Sullivan, Biden Administration National Security Advisor. Speech, April 27th 2023

Chapter Three

1 Robert Lighthizer, 'No Trade is Free' p138
2 Lighthizer p121
3 Lighthizer p122
4 Wolfgang Munchau 'Kaput: The End of the German Miracle' p65-6
5 McGee, Patrick, 'Apple in China: The Capture of the World's Greatest Company' p329
6 McGee p214, p261
7 McGee p310-1
8 McGee p8
9 McGee p10

10 McGee p5
11 McGee p7
12 McGee p5 p271
13 McGee p274
14 McGee p272
15 McGee p273
16 McGee p328-9
17 McGee p330
18 McGee p303-9 p360-1 p379
19 McGee p10 p298
20 McGee p280
21 McGee p371
22 McGee p378
23 McGee p372-4
24 McGee p260
25 Dani Rodrik, 'Straight Talk on Trade' p91
26 Paul Collier 'The Bottom Billion' p82
27 Rodrik p154
28 Rodrik p92

Chapter Four

1 Krueger Anne O. 'International Trade: What Everyone
   Needs to Know' p74-5
2 Hayek, F.A. 'Law Legislation and Liberty' p56

Chapter Six

1 Herrmann, Ulrike, 'The End of Capitalism' p81
2 Herrmann, Ulrike, p73

Bibliography

Acemoglu, Daron, & Johnson, Simon, *Power and Progress: Our Thousand-Year Struggle over Technology and Prosperity*, Basic Books 2023

Bergsten, Clyde, *The United States vs China: The Quest for Global Economic Leadership,* Polity Press 2022

Chang, Ha-Joon, *Bad Samaritans: The Guilty Secrets of Rich Nations, and the Threat to Global Prosperity*, Random House 2007

Cohen, Stephen J. & DeLong, J. Bradford, *The End Of Influence: What Happens When Other Countries Have the Money,* Basic Books 2010

Collier, Paul, *The Bottom Billion: Why the Poorest Countries Are Failing and What Can be Done About It,* Oxford University Press 2008

Gordon, Robert, *The Rise and Fall of American Growth,* Princeton Press 2015

Hayek, F.A. Law, *Legislation, and Liberty*, Routledge and Kegan Paul, various dates, 2013 edition

Henderson, J. Vernon, & Shalizi, Zmarak & Venables, Antony J. *Geography and Development*, World Bank Internet Resource, 1999

Herrmann, Ulrike, *The End of Capitalism: Why Growth and Climate Protection Are Incompatable—and How We Will Live in the Future*, Translation by David Shaw, Verlag, Kiepenheuer & Witsch GmbH & Co. 2025

Hont, Istvan, *Jealousy of Trade: International Competition and the Nation-State in Historical Perspective*, Harvard University Press 2010

Keynes, John Maynard, Collected Works The Macmillan Press, for the Royal Economic Society

Klein, Matthew C., & Pettis, Michael, *Trade Wars are Class Wars: How Rising Inequality Distorts the Global Economy and Threatens International Peace,* Yale University Press 2020

Kruger, Anne O., *International Trade: What Everyone Needs to Know,* Oxford University Press 2020

Lighthizer, Robert, *No Trade is Free: Changing Course, Taking on China, and Helping America's Workers,* Harper Collins 2023

Magnus, George, *Red Flags: Why Xi's China is in Jeopardy*, Yale University Press 2018

McGee, Patrick, *Apple in China: The Capture of the World's Greatest Company,* Simon & Schuster 2025

McMahon, Dinny, *China's Great Wall of Debt: Shadow Banks, Ghost Cities, Massive Loans and the End of the Chinese Miracle,* Little Brown 2018

Movroidis, Petros C. & Andre, Sapir Andre, *China and the WTO: Why Multilateralism Still Matters,* Princeton University Press 2021

Munchau, Wolfgang, *Kaput: The End of the German Miracle,* Swift Press 2024

Oermann, Nils Ole, & Wolff, Hans-Jurgen, *Trade Wars: Past and Present,* Oxford University Press 2022

Prestowitz, Clyde, *Three Billion new Capitalists: The Great Shift of Wealth and Power to the East,* Basic Books 2005

Reinert, Erik S., *How Rich Countries Got Rich ... and Why Poor Countries Stay Poor,* Constable & Robinson Ltd 2007

Rodrik, Dani, *Straight Talk on Trade: Ideas for a Sane World Economy,* Princeton University Press 2018

Shum, Desmond, *Red Roulette: An Insider's Story of Wealth, Power, Corruption, and Vengeance in Today's China*, Simon & Schuster Inc. 2023

Susskind, Daniel, *Growth: A Reckoning*, Penguin Random House 2024

Tucker, Paul, *Global Discord: Values and Power in a Fractured World Order*, Princeton University Press 2022

Wolf, Martin, *The Shifts and the Shocks: What We've Learned – and Have Still to Learn – From the Financial Crisis,* Penguin Group 2014

www.ingramcontent.com/pod-product-compliance
Lightning Source LLC
Chambersburg PA
CBHW031933190326
41519CB00007B/517